THE SOCIAL CATHOLIC MOVEMENT
IN ENGLAND
1920–1955

COMMITTEE IN CHARGE OF CANDIDACY:

Professor Thomas Patrick Neill,
                    Chairman and Adviser
Associate Professor Clarence Leonard Hohl, Jr.
Associate Professor Joseph Aloysius McCallin, S.J.
Associate Professor Edward Joseph Maguire
Professor Kurt Von Schuschnigg

THE SOCIAL CATHOLIC MOVEMENT IN ENGLAND, 1920 - 1955

Sister M. Vivian Brand, P.H.J.C., A.B., A.M., Ph.D.

A Dissertation Presented to the Faculty of the
Graduate School of Saint Louis University
in Partial Fulfillment
of the Requirements for the Degree of
Doctor of Philosophy in History
1963

Pageant Press, Inc.

Published by Pageant Press, Inc.
101 Fifth Avenue, New York, N.Y. 10003

Manufactured in the United States of America.

To
The Sisters of my Community

CONTENTS

PREFACE

Courageous leaders, persons of vision and foresight, have labored zealously, dauntlessly, for the success of the Social Catholic movement in England. Georgiana Putnam Mc-Entee, in her work, *The Social Catholic Movement in Great Britain*, has traced the beginnings of the Movement and the more concerted efforts made in the early twentieth century. It is the purpose of this work to carry the study through the period 1920–1955 and to investigate the dominant areas and undertakings through which the Social Catholic movement endeavored to accomplish its aim of producing a leavening force that would permeate society and direct the political, economic, and social changes and developments along Christian lines.

An introductory chapter gives the historical background to provide the setting for an intensive study of various factors. These include an investigation of (*a*) the attitudes of English Catholics in political and economic crises, involving such issues as wages, strikes, nationalization, labor relations, political parties, social services, and the welfare state; (*b*) various Catholic organizations, their aims, and the means employed to implement them; and (*c*) various Catholic movements, their goals, and the means utilized to achieve them. The study is thus restricted for manageability. While the education question has some relevance to the Social Catholic movement, it is omitted in this work since it is vast enough to constitute a research project in itself. The same is true of the international aspect of the movement.

Primary sources, in the form of the official organs of the various societies, movements, and organizations, as well as publications by leaders in the Social Catholic movement, provided the basic information and material necessary for an adequate study. Secondary sources were employed for background, to substantiate interpretations, and to ascertain attitudes toward, and opinions of, the component elements in the Social Catholic movement. The nature of the problem required the use of the historical method.

Through this study and research the author has incurred a series of obligations. Foremost is the gratitude due to Dr. Thomas P. Neill, faculty adviser, whose competent direction and forbearance made possible this dissertation. To Rev. Joseph A. McCallin, S.J., the writer is indebted for his careful reading of the manuscript in its developing stages. Suggestions made by other committee members are also gratefully acknowledged, and the constant encouragement given by Rev. John Francis Bannon, S.J., director of the department, is sincerely appreciated.

The gracious personnel of the Pius XII Memorial Library, of the St. Louis public libraries, of the Central Bureau of Central Verein Library, and of the Institute of Social Order, where the research was carried on, are gratefully remembered for their assistance. Grateful acknowledgment is due also to particular fellow graduate students who gave continuous encouragement through their sustained interest in the project.

Finally, the writer wishes to express her deep and prayerful gratitude to her religious superiors who provided the opportunity for graduate study and research. For the final typing of the manuscript the writer acknowledges her debt to a fellow sister who obligingly undertook the task. To all companion religious gratitude is also due, for they graciously took upon themselves additional duties during the writer's absence and provided a constant reservoir of spiritual assistance.

THE SOCIAL CATHOLIC MOVEMENT
IN ENGLAND
1920–1955

CHAPTER I

INTRODUCTION

Historical Background

1850–1900. The restoration of the hierarchy in England brought a wild reaction among non-Catholics against what they termed the "papal aggression." Cardinal Wiseman calmed the storm with his telling, forthright *Appeal to the English People*; embarrassed, the press retreated and offered lame excuses for its virulence. Discredited by its show of religious intolerance, the Whig government under Lord Russell, already in controversy over other issues, fell from favor among the English people. The prime minister's success in putting through his Ecclesiastical Titles Bill was anticlimactic as the Church prudently instituted new titles. The issue engendered a political battle of High Churchmen, liberals, and Catholics against ultra-Protestants and die-hards. Incidentally but opportunely, it provided a situation for Catholic intellectuals openly and publicly to defend their position. At Birmingham, John Henry Newman delivered a series of lectures, "Present Position of Catholics," and Cardinal Wiseman himself undertook a series at Southwark. The *Dublin Review* now served an additional purpose,[1] and *The Tablet*,[2] though not always

---

[1] According to J. J. Dwyer, in *The English Catholics, 1850–1950*, ed. George A. Beck (London: Burns, Oates, 1950), p. 475, concerning *The Dublin Review*, Wiseman's ". . . aims were to arouse the torpid Catholic body, to stimulate the Oxford Movement . . . to ensure the co-operation of 'old Catholics' and new converts . . . to put Catholicism on the map."

[2] *The Tablet* was founded in 1840 by Frederick Lucas, **who edited**

1

circumspect in its statements, supplied a sounding board for Catholic opinion. This was a new departure for English Catholics, who until this time remained in the seclusion and silence into which the Reformation had driven them. To the old Catholics[3] this open defense by the New Catholics[4] was foolhardy, and they feared it would incur new oppressive legislation against them. The furor over the Restoration subsided comparatively soon, but due to the government's anti-papal attitude and its abetting of the Liberal forces in the Italian Risorgimento, the English Catholics continued their public defense of Catholicism, which they unfortunately mistakenly identified with the regime in the Papal States. This situation had not yet cleared when the controversy over papal infallibility took on new earnestness due to the calling of the Vatican Council in 1870. During the same period, and continuing even to the present day, the schools question demanded open and frank consideration. Despite the errors and the divisions ensuing among Catholics because of differing opinions on various issues, the fact that the Catholic laity was becoming articulate signified a new assertiveness that, but for other circumstances, might have boded well for the Church in England. As indicated previously, the lay Catholic intellectuals and their followers did not stand alone. Cardinal Wiseman,

it until his death in 1865, when John E. Wallis took the editorship and held it till 1868. Under Wallis it began its conservatism, but Wallis, like Lucas, was guided by personal likes and dislikes. Under Father Herbert Vaughan, 1868–1872, and George Elliot Ranken, 1872–1884, the tone of the paper was much improved, though it still retained a subjectivity. With the editorship of J. G. Snead-Cox, 1884–1920, *The Tablet* became a first-class periodical, a distinction it maintains today. (Beck, *op. cit.*, pp. 482–489) .

[3] The term "old Catholics" as used in this study indicates those Catholics of the Squirearchy who retained the faith from penal times.

[4] The term "new Catholics" refers to those Catholics stemming from the Oxford Movement and converts of approximately the third quarter of the nineteenth century.

having spent the greater part of his early life on the Continent, experienced nothing of the inhibitions of the old Catholics, and was ever ready to participate in and to urge on the vindications. His successor, Cardinal Manning, himself a convert of 1851, though predominantly a man of action, advocated a similar policy of verbal and written apology.

With the passing of the restoration generation, with the internal immigration of many tenants of the Catholic gentry to the industrial centers, with the sons of the squirearchy becoming disciples of Cardinal Newman, and with conversions among the various professions rather than from the elite academic group, an amalgamation of old and new Catholics took place in the last quarter of the nineteenth century. In the fifteenth Duke of Norfolk the period saw the exemplification of a blend of the two groups. Being, ". . . with his brother, (Lord FitzAlan) the last example of the type of the great English Catholic nobleman,"[5] he was at the same time a disciple of Newman, under whom he had been educated. From 1868 to 1917 he ". . . was the lay spokesman of the Catholic body,"[6] and exercised his greatest influence in Catholic affairs during Cardinal Vaughan's year at Westminster. In 1894 he led a group of the laity in drawing up a petition to the bishops requesting ". . . the opening of the universities to Catholics under adequate safeguards."[7] In the following year College of Propaganda approved a bishops' proposal which contained ideas similar to those of the Duke's petition. The perennial elementary schools question also assumed greater significance at this time, and the bishops prevailed upon Cardinal Vaughan and the Duke of Norfolk to broach the

---

[5] David Mathew, *Catholocism in England, 1535–1935* (New York: Longmans, Green and Co., 1936) , p. 232.

[6] George Andrew Beck (ed.), *The English Catholics, 1850–1950* (London: Burns, Oates, 1950), p. 238.

[7] *Ibid.*, p. 307.

subject personally with the Prime Minister, Lord Salisbury, and to ask him ". . . whether the day of discrimination and palliatives should not now give place to the day of justice."[8] The failure of the mission can be traced to dissension among the Anglicans over the issue of voluntary schools rather than to lack of influence on the part of the emissaries. Politically, the Duke of Norfolk was associated with Lord Salisbury, but the only governmental position he held was that of Postmaster General during the years 1895 to 1902—the years of Lord Salisbury's third term as prime minister. This integration of ideas and activities in one man illustrates how, from the end of the nineteenth century, the distinction between old and new Catholics was all but obliterated. Shane Leslie makes the interesting observation that after Manning there were no more convert bishops and that ". . . the Church in England became more and more what it would have been without the intrusion of the Oxford men. The times called for administrators, not national characters, for business organizers, not brilliant controversialists."[9]

A third group of nineteenth-century Catholics must be considered to complete the background of the Church in the twentieth century. Poor Irish immigrants and a few Englishmen constituted this group; they were laborers, wage-earners —approximating a proletariat. They were a vital concern of the Church. By the year of the restoration of the hierarchy, the influx of pauperized victims of the potato famine in Ireland had passed its peak, though immigrants continued to stream into England, converging in the industrial and commercial centers. It was of people of this ilk that Cardinal Wiseman wrote in his *Appeal to the English People*, to vindicate himself against the charge that he would "take over" West-

---

[8] *Ibid.*, p. 382.

[9] *The Oxford Movement, 1833–1933* (Milwaukee: The Bruce Publishing Company, 1933), p. 178.

4

minster Abbey. After extolling the glories of Westminster, he continued:

> Yet this splendid monument, its treasures of art and its fitting endowments, form not the part of Westminster which will concern me. . . . Close under the Abbey of Westminster there lie concealed labyrinths of lanes and courts and alleys and slums, nests of ignorance, vice, depravity and crime, as well as of squalor, wretchedness and disease, in which swarms a huge and countless population, in great measure, nominally at least, Catholic. This is the part of Westminster which alone I covet and which I shall be glad to claim and to visit as a blessed pasture in which sheep of Holy Church are to be tended, in which a bishop's godly work has to be done by consoling, converting and preserving.[10]

Similar conditions prevailed in all the large cities. The shortage of priests to minister to the struggling, half-starved (spiritually and physically) people presented a tremendous problem. Often the English clergy failed to understand these people and their plight. Frequently, this was literally true, for many of the immigrants spoke and understood only the Gaelic language. Irish priests came in greater numbers after 1850, and as the country was organized into dioceses and parishes and missions were established on a planned basis, care of the Catholic poor attained some efficiency. The number of priests, however, remained inadequate despite the increase of missioners and native vocations.

Cardinal Wiseman was alert, too, to the need for care of the children, thousands of whom were in workhouses or in homes where Catholicism was scarcely recognized, and thousands more of whom called the streets home. These conditions constituted a source of England's persistent "leakage" problem. Prior to the restoration, Wiseman had invited religious orders of women to the London vicariate to establish

---

[10] Quoted in Beck, *op. cit.*, p. 517.

orphanages. Shortly after the Cardinal's appointment to Westminster, through his leadership and approval reformatories and industrial schools conducted by priests, brothers, or sisters sprang up throughout the cities of England. For missionary work among the English he founded the order of Oblates of St. Charles, with Father Manning as their head. Under Cardinal Wiseman's successor the policies were continued, for Cardinal Manning, with his acute social sense, was intensely interested in the underprivileged, who were predominantly Irish and Catholic and whom he recognized as ". . . incomparably the most important factor in the Church of England."[11] Yet by the time of Manning's succession, conditions had improved minimally, and whereas previously some schools and Mass houses were provided for the poor out of pity and piety by the traditional Catholics, now the poor contributed from their meager earnings, and schools and churches mushroomed from their pennies.

Their faith was a unifying force affording mutual encouragement through social and economic injustices imposed upon them. Their dogged determination, coupled with the authority given them by the enfranchisement of 1867, gradually brought reforms which made possible a rise from their servile status. From these people came the trade unions and cooperative societies. From these people, too, came leaders in the professions and in politics. Anglo-Irish relations by the turn of the century were becoming increasingly amicable, due in no small measure to Cardinal Manning's sympathetic support on the home rule question and to his beneficent understanding and help in Irish Catholic problems. To him they owed gratitude and respect for tireless efforts in behalf of their religious rights, of Catholic schools, of church building, of temperance, of the Irish laborers seeking justice through the

---

[11] *Ibid.*, p. 279.

labor unions. He had climaxed his endeavors for them in his triumphant efforts in the dock strike of 1889. Truthfully, Manning could state in 1887, "I have spent my life in working for the Irish occupation of England."[12]

The years, as well as intermarriage, had brought assimilation to English life, ways, and customs. In the early twentieth century the Irish still constituted a good proportion of the labor force in England, but they no longer were a class apart. The same can be said of the Irish Catholics; they now belonged to the whole of English Catholics, and their contribution to Catholic leadership had to be taken into account.

1900–1926. In the first quarter of the present century, then, the English Catholics stood as an amalgamation of old Catholics, new Catholics, and Irish Catholics. What role, as such, were they to play in the history of England? Did they constitute a formidable force? Their numerical strength could have made them appear so. The period of Edwardian tolerance and its close contact between Court and Catholics[13] gave the Church greater freedom than it had experienced in England since the Reformation. In 1895 the Church removed the restrictions prohibiting Catholics from attending Oxford and Cambridge. Except for the clergy, however, the first substantial rise in Catholic enrollment occurred only after 1918. With the reign of George V came outright recognition of Catholicism. Among the signatures on the document proclaiming the new King in 1910 were those of prominent Catholics: the Duke of Norfolk, as Earl Marshal of England; Lord Cranard, a Court official as Master of the Horse; Lord Howard Penrith, later Ambassador to Washington; Lord Tyrrel, a former Head of the Foreign Office and ex-Ambassador to Paris; and Lord Justice Greene, an eminent

---

[12] *Ibid.,* p. 265.
[13] Mathew, *op. cit.,* p. 247.

lawyer subsequently appointed to the Privy Council. The King's personal entourage included many Catholics, and his attitude toward the Church was marked by high esteem.[14] Nor were the Catholics lacking in loyalty to the Crown. The outbreak of World War I saw the Irish living in England willing to leave the newly acquired status of home rule inactivated while they, as well as the English, took up arms in defense of the country. Clerical patriotism, too, was evidenced, and from this time the army and navy chaplaincies became permanent institutions with an appointed bishop-in-ordinary having official status at the War Office.[15]

Close Allied relations during the war necessitated the attendance of representatives of the government, of the army and navy, and of the King at various public ceremonies at Westminster Cathedral, which enhanced the prestige of the Church. In 1915 the king re-established diplomatic relations with the Vatican, albeit with much credit to Cardinal Bourne,[16] whose position now differed little from that of the Protestant Archbishop of Canterbury. In fact, by the end of the war, so great had been the change in relations between the Church and the government that "scarcely any national appeal could now be made without referring to the Cardinal Archbishop, as naturally as Governments had always appealed for advice to the Archbishop of Canterbury."[17]

While the two decades spanning the turn of the century had seen converts, especially from Anglicanism, slow to a trickle, so that to many the Church appeared static, the second decade of the new century brought an increase in con-

---

[14] Denis Gwynn, "Catholic England under King George V," *The Catholic World*, CXLIII (April, 1936), 69–70.

[15] *Ibid.*, p. 70.

[16] Mathew, *op. cit.*, p. 241.

[17] Denis Gwynn, "Cardinal Bourne," *The Sign*, XIV (March, 1935), 491.

versions.[18] In the wake of the war days came, too, the usual resurgence of religious fervor. Writing for the *Catholic Who's Who and Year Book 1924*, G. K. Chesterton enthusiastically declared, ". . . the Catholic Church whatever else she is doing, is certainly gaining ground. . . ."[19] Yet there was no pronounced reaction or intense fear by the Protestants at the apparent progress of the Catholic church.

Spirit and Statistics. Gnawing away at the integrity of all religious thought was the materialism born of Charles Darwin's *Origin of Species,* fostered by Thomas Huxley's interpretations, and brought to fruition in the skeptical climate of the early twentieth century. The Church no longer experienced direct outward attack and persecution, but there bored from within by subtle intrusion a pernicious secularism preparatory even for the gross materialism of Communism. Unaware of this penetration, many Catholics became indifferent, individualistic, rallying for group action only when some obvious crisis arose, e.g., in regard to the education question. To characterize the average Catholics of the first quarter of the twentieth century, one can say that in general they were apathetic. Large numbers were Catholics by tradition, rather than by conviction, and knew very little of the tenets of their

---

[18] Most notable were the group conversions: ". . . in 1910 the Brighton vicars were received into the Church and with them a proportion of their two congregations; in 1913 the Anglican community at Caldey under Dom Aelred Carlyle made their submission to the Holy See as did the nuns of St. Bride's Abbey" (*Ibid.,* p. 247). Outstanding individual converts included Donald Attwater, 1910; Eric Gill, 1913; Christopher Dawson, 1914; Compton Mackenzie, 1914; Owen Francis Dudley, 1915; Bruce Marshall, 1918; Ronald Knox, 1919. Gilbert K. Chesterton entered the Church in 1922, but in the preceding decade Catholic thought was prominent in his publications.

[19] Quoted in Georgiana Putnam McEntee, *The Social Catholic Movement in Great Britain* (New York: The Macmillan Company, 1927), p. 9.

9

faith. Furthermore, most of them were oblivious of an apostolic duty as Catholics.

Through the vicissitudes of Catholicism, in the entire period under consideration in this background summary, "leakage" remained a problem for the Church in England. Despite all efforts, conditions to which the "leakage" has been attributed had not been rectified. A shortage of priests persisted, the number of Catholic schools and churches was inadequate, intermarriage continued, mobility of population for job opportunity and thereby frequent loss of contact with other Catholics remained, and permeating all was the growing spirit of secularism and religious liberalism.

As a result of the foregoing attitudes and conditions, the number of Catholics in England by the end of World War I was not, proportionately, what it should have been. Statistics available on the Catholic growth refer to England and Wales. From 1900 onward the figures were published almost yearly, but their reliability can be questioned because of the difficulty in collecting the personal data required and because of the lack of a systematic method in attempting the collection. However, some comparative figures will give an estimate of the relative growth of the Catholic church in England and Wales for approximately the first quarter of the present century. In 1900, Catholics numbered 1,300,000 and in 1921 the estimate was 1,966,000, while the total population for the respective years was 32,678,370 and 38,037,213. The approximate annual average of adult conversions in the years 1900–1925 was 11,000. Clergy, regular and secular, numbered 4,528 in 1925, whereas at the turn of the century their number hovered about 3,000. Public churches and chapels in 1900 totaled 1,500, and by 1925 they had increased to 2,024.[20] As

[20] Statistical information: *Catholic Directory, 1926*; Beck, *op. cit.*, chap. xiv; Joseph Whitaker, *An Almanac for 1961* (London: J. Whitaker and Sons, Ltd.) .

in the nineteenth century, so in the early part of the twentieth there were still large concentrations of Catholics in the cities. The exodus to the suburbs, however, was beginning; and as the century wore on, Catholicism was increasingly represented in all parts of England.[21]

Beginnings of the Social Catholic Movement

Cardinal Manning. The final area to be considered in this background summary relates to some endeavors at amelioration in the social sphere—the seeds and seedlings of the Social Catholic movement in the period 1920–1955. Preeminence in this field in the second half of the nineteenth century belongs rightfully to Cardinal Manning. It was among the laborers, the poor, that he found his special niche of work. To save the faith of these people, Manning perceived the necessity of procuring social justice for them. Prior to any pronouncement of the Church, he spoke out fearlessly against the grasping avarice of the capitalists. While his efforts frequently assumed a negative aspect, in the sense of opposing existing conditions and legislation, or proposed legislation, his aims were actually positive. A lecture, "The Dignity and Rights of Labour," given at Leeds in 1874 revealed his attitude on various issues:

I claim for labour the rights of property . . . the working man carries his property with him as ready money. . . .
Labour has a right to its own freedom, but it has a right to protect itself.
Whatever rights, then, capital possesses, labour possesses.
I am one of those who are of the opinion that the hours of labour must be further regulated by law. . . .
Is it possible for a child to be educated who becomes a half-timer at 10 or even 11 years of age? Is it possible

[21] Beck, *op. cit.,* pp. 423–424.

for a child in the agricultural districts to be educated who may be sent out into the fields at 9? I will ask, can a woman be the mother and head of a family who works sixty hours a week?

The homes of the poor in London are often very miserable. The state of the houses—families living in single rooms, sometimes many families in one room, a corner apiece. These things cannot go on; . . .[22]

But Manning was primarily a man of action: hence, theory was a guide to practical achievement, not an end in itself. Accordingly, wherever he found organizations—international or national, state, religious, or private—through which he could help to relieve the suffering of the poor or ameliorate social conditions, he became an active participant.[23] Philanthropic works and programs benefited and were furthered by his personal charity. His interest in the care and rescue of children, especially in regard to their religious training and proper education, put him in the vanguard of opposition or proposition, as the situation dictated, for legislation on the schools question. He founded the Westminster Diocesan Education Fund and within fourteen years could say, "There is school room for all."[24] He worked in close harmony with the Voluntary Schools Association founded in 1884 by Herbert Vaughan,[25] and his interest in the education of youth was ". . . given official recognition when he was made one of the members of the royal commission appointed by the queen to inquire into and report upon the whole subject of primary education."[26] For the welfare of the children, Manning con-

[22] Henry Edward Manning, *Miscellanies,* Vol. II (London: Burns and Oates, 1877), pp. 81–97.

[23] McEntee, *op. cit.,* p. 40.

[24] Beck, *op. cit.,* p. 158.

[25] Ernest Edwin Reynolds, *Three Cardinals* (New York: P. J. Kenedy & Sons, 1958), p. 254.

[26] McEntee, *op. cit.,* p. 45.

tinually agitated to raise the minimum age for child labor. The investigations of the commission supported his contentions and ". . . had proved that the half-time system hindered the acquisition of knowledge, disrupted the discipline of the schools and lowered their moral tone."[27]

Perhaps Cardinal Manning's best-known work was in behalf of temperance. Drunkenness among the poor he saw as the source of ruination of communities and families as well as of individuals. His League of the Cross tolerated no halfway measures; all members were pledged to total abstinence. Annually the league met at the Crystal Palace, with Manning at the forefront of all its plans and activities. Its crusading enthusiasm was stimulated through the Cardinal's zeal and through his efforts to procure legislation banning the liquor traffic, which, though lucrative for the government, was destroying the nation.

Mention has already been made of Manning's interest in the laboring class and his work on behalf of their rights. As early as 1872 he was defending the workers' right to association for protection. In commenting on the archbishop's speech made at a meeting of the Agricultural Labourers' Union, Mr. Arch, a pioneer of trade unions, indicated the prelate's influence: He ". . . spoke up nobly for us. The testimony . . . of a man so respected was of the greatest value to the union."[28] He approved of the "new unionism" under the leadership of John Burns and Ben Tillett. With them and the dock directors he negotiated the settlement of the dock strike in 1889.

Every phase of the workers' life and the problems involved drew the Cardinal's attention. He supported the Shop Hours League, and in time of employment "declared that

---

[27] *Ibid.*, p. 49.
[28] Quoted in Shane Leslie, *Cardinal Manning* (New York: P. J. Kenedy & Sons, 1954), p. 150.

'every man has a right to work or to bread.' "[29] The grossly inadequate housing of the poor was his constant concern, and governmental acknowledgment of Manning's social work was again demonstrated when he was appointed to the Royal Commission on the Housing of the Working Classes.[30] The preceding examples of his good works indicate his multifarious interests. In Leo XIII's encyclical *Rerum Novarum*, Cardinal Manning saw the crowning of his labors. It substantiated his theories and his attempts at securing their practical application. It was an official pronouncement on the Church's social responsibilities, and Manning valued the encyclical ". . . as the most profound expression of social justice since the words spoken in the wilderness: 'I have compassion on the multitude.' "[31]

Other Leaders. Two other prelates must be mentioned as forerunners of the Social Catholic Movement of the twentieth century. Edward Gilpin Bagshawe, Bishop of Nottingham from 1874 to 1901, pioneered in theory on social justice rather than in action. His pastoral letters of 1883 and 1884 indicated his thinking was far in advance of his time, and he was quickly branded socialistic. The living wage, rights of labor, proper housing, duties of the state were aspects of the social question on which he expressed opinions strikingly similar to those in Leo XIII's *Rerum Novarum*.[32]

In Louis Charles Casartelli, Bishop of Salford from 1903 to 1925, the worker found another champion of social justice. He approved the cooperative movement as a means of eradicating the social ills resulting from industrialism.[33] Under his leader-

---

[29] Reynolds, *op. cit.,* p. 253.

[30] *Ibid.,* p. 251.

[31] Beck, *op. cit.,* p. 27.

[32] J. M. Cleary, *Catholic Social Action in Britain 1909–1959* (Oxford: Catholic Social Guild, 1961), pp. 20–21; McEntee, *op. cit.,* pp. 299–301.

[33] McEntee, *op. cit.,* p. 162.

14

ship organized Catholic action, clergy and laity working together, made its debut as the Salford Diocesan Federation. Its activity was short-lived—halted by political complications—but nominally it existed for almost twenty-five years. From it there developed the National Conference of Catholic Trade Unionists,[34] to which Philip Hughes attributes a considerable influence: ". . . in the struggle to keep the parliamentary Labour Party—to which the Conference was affiliated—a non-Socialist body." He continues, "The National Conference came to an abrupt end when the Labour Party 'socialized' its constitution in 1918."[35] The main purpose of the Federation was summed up by the same author:

> . . . it was definitely meant to train Catholics in active participation in whatever party their interest in public affairs prompted them to join. The plan was to inform the Catholic with Catholic social teaching, and with a judgment based on Catholic principles about all the practical questions of the day, and to send him thus informed into local public life.[36]

The contributions of others, including the laymen Charles Stanton Devas and Mrs. Virginia Crawford, to Catholic social thought could be reviewed, but the foregoing illustrates the ground preparation and the seed sown by individual efforts. Unfortunately, no perpetuating plan had been devised to carry on the work so nobly begun in charity guided by a keen, personal sense of social justice. It provided inspiration, but the social question now presented a challenge that called for concerted action. Michael P. Fogarty adeptly appraised the situation:

> *Rerum Novarum* marked a turning point, it did not create one. Like all the Papal social encyclicals, it represented

---

[34] *Ibid.*, p. 205.
[35] Beck, *op. cit.*, p. 39.
[36] Quoted in Cleary, *op. cit.*, p. 30.

15

the summing up of a certain stage of thought and discussion about social problems among Catholics, both clerical and lay. A picture of new problems and solutions was emerging from this discussion. A transition was under way from one major stage in the growth of Christian Democracy to another. *Rerum Novarum* represented the turn of the screw which brought one part of the new picture finally into focus.[37]

In answer to the challenge, the following Continental example, some small but significant organizations developed—seedlings of a planned social Catholic movement.

Catholic Social Guild. Foremost among these organizations was the Catholic Social Guild. It was founded in 1909 by a group of persons who were like-minded concerning social conditions and the role of the Church: Monsignor Henry Parkinson (who became the first President), James Britten (co-founder of the Catholic Truth Society), Father Michael Maher, S.J., Dr. A. P. Mooney, Hubert Hull, Dom Lambert Nolle, Father J. Lomax, George Eliot Ansthruther, William Byrne, Bertrand Devas, Miss Ada Streeter, Mrs. Philip Gibbs, Miss Margaret Fletcher, and Mrs. Virginia Crawford, under the instigation and leadership of Father Charles Dominic Plater, S.J., and Leslie Toke.[38] Each founder-member was to play an important role in the Guild's development by writing, speech, and action. The plan and purpose of the new organization was explained at one of the public gatherings of the Catholic Truth Society Conference, and endorsement of the hierarchy was given by the attending bishops. A few weeks later the appointed committee members: Monsignor Parkinson, Father Plater, Virginia Crawford, James Britten, Leslie Toke, and Bertrand Devas met at Oscott, where they produced the first statutes, named the organization the Catholic

---

[37] *Christian Democracy in Western Europe 1820–1953* (Notre Dame, Indiana: University of Notre Dame Press, 1957), p. 342.
[38] Cleary, *op. cit.,* pp. 10–11.

Social Guild, and stated its objective as "to facilitate intercourse between Catholic students and workers."[39]

In 1910 the Guild made its first public appearance at the National Catholic Congress held at Leeds. Ten months after its inception Monsignor Parkinson could report a membership of 263 persons. Expansion of the organization, in terms of members and activities, was simultaneous. A guild pamphlet[40] containing the statutes as revised in 1912 listed its objectives as:

(a) To facilitate intercourse between Catholic students and workers,
(b) To assist in working out the application of Catholic principles to actual social conditions,
(c) To create a wider interest among Catholics in social questions, and to secure their co-operation in promoting social reform on Catholic lines.
Note: The Guild takes no part in party politics.

Subsequent to this a paragraph entitled "Means" stated:

The Guild endeavours to secure its ends by promoting systematic and concerted study, by the production and circulation of literature dealing with social subjects, by supplying information, by encouraging the training and provision of lecturers, and generally by co-operation with local social effort.[41]

These means were extensively utilized. The "systematic and concerted study" was directed primarily through the study club. This plan was not original, and Father O'Hea stated, ". . . if the Guild took its ideas from Catholic movements abroad, its methods were also stimulated by the rise of adult education and the coming of the Workers' Educational As-

---

[40] *The Catholic Social Guild; What It Is and What It Does* (n.p. and n.d. given; the contents indicate 1913 or 1914 as the year).
[41] *Ibid.*, p. 30.
[39] *Ibid.*, p. 36.

17

sociation and the University Tutorial Classes."[42] The immediate success and the rapid development of the study club system indicated the need for, and interest in, such a movement among wage earners who constituted the membership. In 1911, there were sixteen study clubs in England and Wales with a total of 171 members; in 1914, ninety-five study clubs were in existence with membership at approximately one thousand. Seventy-eight were concentrated in northern England, while the remaining were scattered through southern England and Wales. It was evident that the study club was becoming a dominant activity of the Guild—a development unforeseen by the founders.[43] Furthermore, other organizations, such as the diocesan federations and the Catholic Young Men's Society, adopted the system; and priests and religious, too, had their circles.[44] Apparently the clubs were becoming a vital means of fulfilling the aim of the Social Catholic movement to permeate society and to direct it along Christian principles.

Problems accompanied the unexpected growth. Adequately equipped leaders for the clubs were sadly lacking. Parish priests undertook the task in many instances, but their number was insufficient. The dire financial status of the Guild prohibited an ample supply of books for the study groups. Finally, it was hard-pressed to provide study plans, courses, and examinations. The clubs proceeded apace despite all obstacles, and having survived the upheaval of World War I, their number increased to 127 by 1921, and they were described as

Little groups of Catholic working-men students, buying their own textbooks, paying subscriptions to the Guild,

[42] Leo O'Hea, S.J., "The Catholic Social Guild," *The Sword of the Spirit*, Bulletin Number 59 (July 8, 1943), 7.

[43] McEntee, *op. cit.*, p. 191.

[44] McEntee, *op. cit.*, p. 191.

struggling patiently to acquire Catholic knowledge for themselves, unaided by personal contact with a teacher, they yet attained educational results not inferior to those of the liberally-financed tutorial classes which have the government, the universities and the trade unions at their back.[45]

In the adult educational program the Guild also inaugurated correspondence tuition. For schools that wished to initiate social studies it provided study plans adapted to the secondary level. Through the latter, the Guild attempted to penetrate a social stratum above that of the wage earner.

The guild planned and prepared syllabuses, some textbooks, and examinations for the various groups; diplomas were awarded to successful candidates. The courses covered three broad areas: economic theory, the social and economic history of England, and some social problems of the day, such as the living wage and sweated labor. A basic text preferred by study clubs for many years was Monsignor Parkinson's *Primer of Social Science,* published in 1913. Supplementary reading material was provided through the "book boxes." These were supplied, on loan, by the Catholic Truth Society. Georgiana Putnam McEntee gives a general description of the "boxes":

One type of box will contain an assortment of standard general works, a collection of specialised volumes on various social problems,—Trade Unionism, or Woman's Work and Wages, for example; and to these books, usually the work of non-Catholics, are added a few written from a distinctly Catholic standpoint. Sometimes the whole set of over twenty books deals with a particular subject which some study club may be considering, such as Socialism or International Relations. . . . Works of a purely political nature and those representing extreme viewpoints on the social question are generally avoided.[46]

---

[45] Quoted in Cleary, *op. cit.,* p. 66.
[46] *Op. cit.,* p. 189.

19

Carrying out its projected "Means," the Guild trained and provided lecturers. The founding members themselves went their separate ways on tours at various times of the year. Through the study clubs new lecturers were prepared. Their scope, however, was generally limited to ". . . meetings called to promote Study Clubs."[47] They explained the need for social study and, having been members of study clubs, showed how they should be formed. In addition, each lecturer was prepared to speak on one or two specific topics pertaining to the social question. Lists indicating the persons and their subjects were available at the Catholic Social Guild Headquarters.[48]

A dearth of literature on Catholic principles and views regarding the social question, and the aim "To create a wider interest among Catholics in social questions, and to secure their co-operation in promoting social reform on Catholic lines," prompted the leading members of the Guild to write extensively. The *Quarterly Bulletin,* issued regularly from mid-1911 through 1920, kept members and all readers abreast of the Guild's aims, activities, and achievements. Its provocative articles called attention to social problems; its reviews aroused interest in available literature on social problems; and its news on projected social legislation alerted readers to Parliamentary action. The *Catholic Social Year Book* was considered a "must" to recount social progress at home and abroad. After five years it was decided to devote the Yearbook to a special topic. Accordingly, the book for 1916 was entitled *National Reconstruction;* that of 1917, *Catholics in England, Their Needs and Opportunities;* and the 1918 issue, *Christian Social Crusade.* Following the tenth anniversary number, which again reviewed the organization's achievements and indicated its goals for the future, the books reverted to the

---

[47] *Catholic Social Year Book, 1920* (Oxford: Catholic Social Guild) , p. 95.
[48] *Ibid.* This page gives one such list.

specific topic plan. Numerous timely penny pamphlets[49] expounding social principles were published in conjunction with the Catholic Truth Society. More extensive and more enduring in quality was the series *Catholic Studies in Social Reform,* which became the manuals used by the study clubs. Further listing would indicate the prolific output of the Catholic Social Guild in its early years; the quality of many of the larger works is attested by the repeated editions and revisions required by the continued demand for them.[50]

Even in its first decade the Catholic Social Guild attempted to work with and through other existing organizations, whether they were Catholic, nondenominational, or interdenominational; local, national, or international. In this the Guild followed the exhortation of Cardinal Bourne given in a speech at the National Catholic Congress at Leeds in 1910:

> Catholics will, then, be acting in accordance with the traditions left them by the second Archbishop [Manning], if, as members of Municipal Bodies or as Guardians of the Poor or by consenting to act on the various committees to promote national objects, they give their time and talent to the service of the common good of our country . . . they will often have the opportunity of friendly cooperation with various bodies, which, though not Catholic in origin or in name, yet are in no way hostile to the Catholic Church, but are on the contrary sincerely anxious to have the support and experience which Catholics can give.[51]

---

[49] The series of penny pamphlets for 1910, 1912, and 1914 respectively are listed in Patricia Barrett, R.S.C.J., "The Social Catholic Movement in England from 1850 to 1940" (unpublished Master's thesis, Graduate School, Saint Louis University, 1940), p. 35.

[50] A more extensive review of Catholic Social Guild literature is given in McEntee, *op. cit.,* pp. 183–189. Cleary, *op. cit., passim,* cites lists for various periods and topics.

[51] Quoted in Cleary, *op. cit.,* p. 75.

Catholic societies were affiliated with the Catholic Social Guild on a membership basis. Their actual interest was shown by the formation of study clubs and their calls for lecturers from the guild's rosters. In November, 1910, such affiliations numbered seventeen; a year later the number was thirty-six. The Catholic federations of various dioceses co-operated with the guild also, and that of Westminster at its council meeting in 1911 urged "that the objects and work of the Catholic Social Guild be brought under the notice of all our Branches . . ." and that "the Women's Catholic Federation . . . apply for membership of the Catholic Social Guild."[52] Some prominent charter members of the Guild were charter members also of the Catholic Women's League, founded in 1906 by Miss Margaret Fletcher ". . . to secure unified action among Catholic lay women for the furthering of religious and intellectual interest and the promotion of social work."[53] Miss Fletcher wrote extensively and, like Mrs. Crawford, contributed some of the most valuable literature the Guild published.[54] Miss Ada Streeter, first Honorary Secretary of the Catholic Women's League, for many years was correspondence tutor in economics for the Catholic Social Guild.[55] In reality, the two organizations had some common goals, and for their work to be effective cooperation was almost inevitable.

A prestige-bearing contact was that with the British Institute of Social Service. Among its vice-presidents were Cardinal Bourne and Sidney Webb, and its committee included a representative of the Catholic Social Guild. Nondenominational societies that covered vast and varied areas of social work were

[52] *Catholic Social Year Book, 1912,* p. 20.
[53] McEntee, *op. cit.,* p. 238.
[54] *Ibid.,* p. 178.
[55] "Notes and Comments," *The Christian Democrat,* XX (October, 1940), 148.

22

recommended to all Catholics for cooperation to make known, and bring action along, Catholic principles. The *Catholic Social Year Book, 1917,* commenting on the Workers' Educational Association, cites an example of the possible influence of Catholics: "One of their study clubs which is attended by two C.S.G. members has agreed not to pass any judgment on Catholic questions until the Catholic members have had a chance of stating their case."[56] Acknowledgment of the guild's work was given by the repeated requests for representatives to attend public meetings and conferences.[57]

Interdenominational cooperation of the guild is illustrated particularly by its participation in the Swanwick Summer Schools. Here, under the title "Interdenominational Conference of Social Service Unions," several organizations—including, in 1912, Catholic Social Guild, Christian Social Union, Congregational Social Service Committee, National Conference Union for Social Service, Primitive Methodist Social Service Union, Presbyterian Social Service Union, United Methodist Social Service Union, Society of Friends Social Union, and the Wesleyan Methodist Union for Social Service —met ". . . to discuss social problems on which agreement was possible and discussion would be fruitful. . . ."[58] From 1912 to 1916, the central themes of the meetings were "The Life of the Industrial Worker," "The Industrial Unrest and the Living Wage," "Land and Labour," "International Relationships," and "Social Reconstruction After the War." Father Plater's program of social reform, drawn up on request, was accepted by ten of the most important religious denominations and ". . . became the basis for the I.C.S.S.U. joint statement on 'Christian Social Reconstruction.' "[59] Until Father

[56] p. 65.
[57] *Catholic Social Year Book, 1919,* p. 32.
[58] *Ibid.,* p. 29.
[59] Cleary, *op. cit.,* p. 77.

23

Plater's death there was also official cooperation of the Catholic Social Guild with the Conference on Christian Politics, Economics, and Citizenship.[60] The guild was well represented on the Temperance Council of the Christian Churches, and Cardinal Bourne frequently requested Father O'Hea to attend other interdenominational meetings that were concerned with the social question.[61]

International contact marked the Catholic Social Guild from its inception. Continental Catholic Social organizations, such as the Frauenbund and the Volksverein of Germany and the Action Populaire of France had served as models for the English Social Catholic movement. In the years 1909 to 1911 Père Cavrois, delegate of Action Populaire, spoke at the Guild's annual meeting. In 1913 Mrs. Crawford was the Guild's representative to the Antwerp International Congress organized by the Ligues Sociales d'Acheters. As a matter of policy the early Yearbooks contained a review of Social Catholic achievements abroad, and there were contributions from the pens of Continental leaders. Prior to World War I the seed of the Catholic Social Guild was sown in Australia through Archibishop Mannix, and study clubs were established in New Zealand. Contact with Canada was rooted in Montreal and Toronto through the efforts of Henry Somerville, an enthusiastic guild member and leader since his meeting with Father Plater in 1910 at Leeds. Guild members lectured in America and contributed to its magazines; Guild publications in American editions found a ready sale.[62] A series of publications on the law of nations, at the end of the war, served one aspect of the Guild's international work that had repercussions through the 1920's and 1930's in the support of the

---

60 *Ibid.*
61 *Ibid.*
62 *Catholic Social Year Book, 1919*, pp. 36–37.

League of Nations[63] and in the peace efforts of English Catholics.[64]

Informative Organizations. An informative organization predating the Catholic Social Guild was the Catholic Truth Society. Though it existed for a brief period prior to 1872, the Catholic Truth Society as it is known today was officially founded in 1884 by Bishop Vaughan in conjunction with a group of priests and laymen, inspired by James Britten, who had already begun the work. The aims of the Society are specifically stated as:

> . . . the spreading, among Catholics, of small devotional works, and, among Protestants, of information concerning the Catholic faith and practises; the aiding of the uneducated poor in obtaining a better knowledge of their religion; and the promoting of the circulation of good and inexpensive Catholic literature.[65]

The church-door box and the Box-tenders Association provided a considerable impetus to dissemination of the literature. While the Society strove to fulfill its goals, it soon developed an intense interest in the social question. Lecturing on social problems and Catholic principles became a recognized activity. Among those pioneering in this venture were Monsignor Parkinson, Dr. Mooney, Leslie Toke, Virginia Crawford, and Father Plater.[66] *The Catholic Social Year Book, 1912* recorded that within the past year the ". . . Society's Organizing Secretary [Mr. G. E. Ansthruther] had addressed about 100 meetings in different parts of England . . . at which the audiences have been composed mainly of

---

63 Cleary, *op. cit.,* p. 74.
64 McEntee, *op. cit.,* p. 282.
65 "Catholic Truth Society," *The New Catholic Dictionary,* eds. Conde B. Pallen and John J. Wayne, S.J. (1929), p. 184.
66 Cleary, *op. cit.,* p. 32.

working men and women."[67] Many of its publications dealt with aspects of the social question, and by the turn of the century social problems held a significant place in the society's annual conference.[68] It was at the conference of 1909 that the Catholic Social Guild came into being when the group of interested persons met at a luncheon and formulated the plan. J. M. Cleary states, appropriately, "If his [Father Plater's] idea was the pearl, then the C.T.S. has some claim to be the oyster."[69] It fostered the Catholic Social Guild by publishing its pamphlets, outlines, Yearbooks, and soon in its first years, by advertising it in its own publications, and by devoting some pages to guild affairs in each issue of its official organ, *Catholic Book Notes*. This additional interest of the society did not subvert its original purpose, which it continued to serve despite financial difficulties.

At Westminster in 1918, the Catholic Evidence Guild, another informative organization, was founded. It differed from the preceding organizations in that its aim was, and remained, the teaching of the Catholic religion—its doctrines, its practices—to non-Catholics. Regarding Catholics, the guild endeavored to develop their apostolic spirit and to recruit speakers and other member-workers from among them.[70] The method of teaching was original in that it was done by outdoor preaching, usually at a prominent part of the city. Although it is a lay organization, the clergy occasionally have taken the "pitch." In England, from its earliest days, Father Vincent McNabb, O.P. and Father Hugh Pope, O.P., were familiar figures at Marble Arch.[71] The Guild is organized on diocesan

[67] p. 51.

[68] McEntee, *op. cit.*, pp. 158–168, *passim.*

[69] *Op. cit.*, pp. 32–33.

[70] James Byrne, "Catholic Evidence Guild," *The Catholic Encyclopedia*, XVII, Supplement I (1922), p. 165.

[71] Beck, *op. cit.*, pp. 465, 466.

lines, and its activity is under the close direction of the bishop. Speaking precisely, the Catholic Evidence Guild has no relation to the social question:

> The Guild has a very essential rule, and that is the entire exclusion of politics from its platform. . . . The rule is extended in practice to the avoidance of controversial questions of a social and economic nature, which though not strictly political yet might easily distract the meeting from its true aim, which is religious.[72]

From the beginning, adherence to this rule was rigid. Nevertheless, the Catholic Evidence Guild had its bearing on the Social Catholic Movement, for it helped to remove prejudice and clarified misrepresentations of Catholicism.

Charitable Organizations. In addition to the social and informative organizations there were numerous charitable groups, both lay and religious. While these worked to minimize and alleviate the sufferings of the poor, the sick, prisoners, and such, they were not, strictly speaking, a direct part of the Social Catholic Movement. This is not to demean the societies and their ministrations, for as Henry Somerville stated, "Their activities are of the highest social value. . . ."[73] However, "They are a part of the social movement only in so far as they cooperate with the government or other public bodies, to carry out what is recognized as a policy of the society. . . ."[74] If, then, a charitable society cooperates with the authority in a particular area, if it adapts itself to the policy of that authority, if it attempts to influence that policy or seeks to inculcate Catholic principles, then it takes on a social dimension. Many societies frequently cross into the

---

[72] Henry Browne, S.J., *The Catholic Evidence Movement* (London: Burns, Oates & Washbourne, Ltd., 1921), p. 60.

[73] "The Catholic Social Movement in England," *The Catholic Charities Review,* XIII (March, 1929), 81.

[74] *Ibid.*

social field, though it may not be an avowed policy to do so. Through their charity these societies accomplish a ground-work of dispelling prejudice and thereby are of direct assistance to the Social Catholic movement. The St. Vincent de Paul Society, The Ladies of Charity, The Catholic Needlework Guild, and The Catholic Prisoners' Aid Society are but a few of the charitable organizations founded in the nineteenth century and continuing their services in the twentieth century.

The Social Catholic movement in the period 1920–1955 was built on its past plans and achievements, some of which have been indicated above. To continue and enlarge the good work required but a branching out and a flowering of existing organizations and movements. How the Social Catholic movement actually proceeded will be considered in the succeeding chapters.

Chapter II

ATTITUDE OF ENGLISH CATHOLICS IN POLITICAL SITUATIONS AND ECONOMIC CRISES

England's between-the-wars period, its war years, and its postwar era brought economic, social, and political situations and crises that required unprecedented skill, tact, and understanding in trying to meet the demands of the times and of the people. Schemes, plans, and programs of multi-political shades, of varied economic systems, and of diverse social policies were presented and initiated. To all these the Social Catholic movement responded—sometimes approving and advocating, at other times criticizing and denouncing, but withal setting forth the Catholic principles requisite for social justice. Generally speaking, no group or organization within the Social Catholic movement presented specific plans or programs. The aim was to produce a leavening force that would permeate society and direct the political, economic, and social changes along lines consistent with the principles emphasized in the social pronouncements of the Holy See. To what extent the movement achieved its aim is difficult to ascertain. Occasional differences of opinion among the Catholics undoubtedly were detrimental to the cause. However, some of the basic principles advocated were at times embodied in new legislation. One suspects this was not always done by mere chance. The principles were constantly reiterated in the official organs and by lecturers sponsored by groups in the Social Catholic movement. Furthermore, the concentration on them in study clubs; the adoption of them by some Protestant organizations and by labor groups, which usually counted a substantial Catholic representation; and by other societies constituted a force that the government could not consistently and profitably ignore.

Mining Crises and Relevant Issues

In the wake of World War I there remained many problems to which the upheaval had brought no solutions; on the contrary, some situations were seriously aggravated. One such problem was the perennial English coal mining and coal miners' condition. Since it involved so many basic principles of social justice, it will be studied in this investigation as the focal point of a consideration of Catholic attitudes toward economic crises.

Wages. During the war the government had imposed a measure of control over the coal industry in order to stabilize it. The end of the war brought the prospect of a return to prewar conditions. Prior to the actual withdrawal of government control, the miners took up their cry for nationalization, with some worker control, and for a guaranteed minimum wage. The latter had been advocated by the Catholic Social Guild as a general principle of social justice for some years. In 1921 the organization published its first specific platform, which comprised four areas of interest:

1. The Maintenance and Defence of the Christian Family. . . .
2. The Establishment of a Living Wage as the Universal minimum Wage. . . .
3. Partnership instead of Class Antagonism in Industry. . . .
4. The Diffusion of Property. . . .[1]

The "plank" regarding the minimum wage, then, indicated a

[1] "What We Are," *The Christian Democrat,* I (January, 1921), 2–3.

new aspect—that of a living wage. This was in keeping with *Rerum Novarum*, which advocated not merely a subsistence wage but one that is ". . . sufficient to enable him [the workman] to maintain himself, his wife, and his children in reasonable comfort, . . . and . . . to put by some little savings."[2] A year later the Guild espoused the cause of the family wage system based on the French family allowances plan. In article upon article for the subsequent ten years Henry Somerville expounded and recommended the plan, particularly in the pages of *The Christian Democrat*.[3] Among Catholics, as well as among others in England, there was a general apathy toward the plan. However, it did not lack publicity, as the following comment indicates:

> The Family Wage System . . . is becoming widely known through the efforts of Miss E. Rathbone and The Family Endowment Council. The rapid spread of the movement to many industries and in many countries has given a body of successful experience that should lead to a demand for its consideration in England.[4]

Despite this early optimistic outlook, it was only after World War II that the government of England took cognizance of the plan and acted upon it. In the meantime, the campaign for its adoption was carried on; the Archbishop of Liverpool, President of the Catholic Social Guild, stated unequivocally, "So long as private enterprise can fulfil its primary social func-

---

2 Anne Freemantle (ed.), *The Papal Encyclicals* (New York: The New American Library, 1956), p. 187.

3 Cleary, *op. cit.*, p. 115, n.

4 "Notes and Comments," *The Christian Democrat*, IV (March, 1924), 38.

In 1924 Miss Elinore Rathbone published her book *The Disinherited Family*, which advocated the plan on either an employer or national basis. Her continued efforts on behalf of the system culminated in another book, *The Case for Family Allowances*, published in 1940.

tion of providing a family wage for those necessitous millions, it can justify its existence. When it fails in its primary social function, it stands self-condemned. . . ."[5] Lecturing at a meeting held at Sodality Hall, Farm Street, on March 24, 1933, Father Lewis Watt emphasized the importance of a settlement of the wage problem: "If this question of a just wage were not settled, said Father Watt, nothing would prevent a social and economic revolution."[6] In a series of lectures elucidating *Rerum Novarum* and *Quadragesimo Anno*, E. J. Coyne again stressed the necessity of the family living wage; by it alone could the proletarianism of the workman be ended. *Quadragesimo Anno* advocated a reconstruction of society to generate such reform.[7]

Strikes. When, in 1921, contrary to the recommendations of the Sankey Commission,[8] the government withdrew its con-

[5] Frederick W. Keating, "A Family Living Wage," *The Christian Democrat,* VI (July, 1926), 106.

[6] "Orbis Terrarum," *The Tablet,* CLXI (April 1, 1933), 414.

[7] "Catholic Social Doctrine and Modern Problems," *The Tablet,* CLXIV (October 6, 1934), 437–438.

[8] In 1919 the government established a commission under Mr. Justice Sankey to investigate the mines problem. The thirteen members disagreed in their recommendations and finally submitted four separate reports, thereby intensifying the difficulty of the government, which had pledged itself to accept the report. There was no majority report, but a majority did favor nationalization and all members approved government ownership of the coal measures. However, "Sir Arthur Duckham issued a separate report proposing unification under private profits and a degree of price control" (William W. Haynes, *Nationalization in Practice* [Boston: Harvard University, 1953], p. 25). This last the government proposed to follow, but in a modified form. Opposition on the part of the miners precipitated the strike, and eventually the government abandoned its scheme; but the miners ultimately were defeated and submitted to wage cuts as well as increased hours. For a brief discussion see Haynes, *op. cit.,* pp. 24–26, and G. D. H. Cole and Raymond Postgate, *The British People 1746–1946* (New York: Alfred A. Knopf, 1947), pp. 461–463.

trol, making wages cuts and the eight-hour day imminent, the miners resorted to strike action, abetted by the Social Catholic movement. The editor of *The Month* stated the general attitude toward the situation:

> ... the miners are standing out, at terrible cost to themselves and their dependents, for human conditions of living, and in this they have with them the Christian reformer, whose attitude toward the whole of this question is regulated by three principles, viz., that the first charge upon an industry is the decent support of those who maintain it, that the law should protect from exploitation those workers who cannot protect themselves, and that those engaged in the basic industry of coal-mining should be treated with consideration corresponding to their importance to the welfare of the State.[9]

On behalf of the Catholic Social Guild, Monsignor Parkinson, President, and Henry Somerville, Secretary, signed a manifesto supporting the miners' case.[10] Approval of the planned sympathy strike of the other members of the Triple Alliance, the railwaymen and the transport workers, was given also. Swift denunciation followed the withdrawal of the strike order:

> The nation has escaped the calamity of a general strike, but not through a triumph of reason and moderation. The Triple Alliance leaders who cancelled the strike order did so frankly to save their own organization, though they believed that the miners' cause was a just one. No trade unionist can look back upon the episode without shame.[11]

Endorsement of strike action, under justifiable condi-

---

[9] "Topics of the Month," *The Month,* CXXXVII (May, 1921), 460.

[10] Cleary, *op. cit.,* p. 116.

[11] Notes and Comments," *The Christian Democrat,* I (May, 1921), 4.

tions,[12] was maintained as a policy of the Social Catholic movement. The Catholic Social Guild was particularly sedulous in supporting it, hoping thereby to bring about some social justice. In 1926 it sanctioned the general strike.[13] This was occasioned by the sympathy strike action of the Trades Union Congress to protest, with the miners, the withdrawal of the government subsidy which had maintained a minimum wage for the miners. To the great chagrin of the Catholic

---

[12] "The following conditions are required to justify a strike: (1) a just cause; (2) the fruitlessness of peaceful means, such as conciliation, arbitration, etc., which must be resorted to as a first recourse, so far as possible; (3) a reasonable proportion between the injuries inflicted and the good to be secured; (4) a solid hope of success to be achieved ultimately, at least, by the workers. A just contract, observed by employer, may not be violated." Joseph Husslein, S.J., *Social Wellsprings* (Milwaukee: The Bruce Publishing Company, 1940), I, p. 190, n.

[13] From August, 1925 to March, 1926 the Royal Commission on the Coal Industry, under the chairmanship of Sir Herbert Samuel, conducted its investigation. "It recommended nationalization of royalties, the acceleration of amalgamation, and the establishment of cooperative selling agencies, as well as benefits for the miners, such as joint pit committees, profit-sharing schemes, better housing, and pithead baths" (Haynes, *op. cit.*, p. 30). At the time of the Commission's report ". . . the state of feeling between the colliery-owners and the mineworkers was such that the Government decided that it was useless to attempt to enforce the recommendations of the Commission as a whole" (William H. B. Court, *Coal* [London: His Majesty's Stationery Office and Longmans, Green and Co., 1951], pp. 12–13). The general strike lasted nine days, but the miners remained out for six months. Theirs was a lost cause, and they returned to work accepting wage cuts without a minimum, and longer hours. According to Court, "National negotiation disappeared; it was not until 1936 that the establishment of the Joint Standing Consultative Committee of owners and men, with power to discuss all questions of common interest, not excluding general principles applicable to determination of wages under district negotiations, appeared to acknowledge that the purely district view was becoming out of date. The question of the minimum did not become practical politics again until the Second World War" (*Op. cit.*, p. 13).

Social Guild, Francis Cardinal Bourne, from the pulpit of Westminster Cathedral, condemned the general strike in no uncertain terms. The strike had begun on May third; on May ninth the Cardinal stated:

It is necessary that Catholics should have clearly before their minds the moral principles which are involved:—
(1) There is no moral justification for a general strike of this character. It is a direct challenge to lawfully constituted authority and inflicts, *without adequate reason,* immense discomfort and injury on millions of our fellow-countrymen. It is, therefore, a sin against the obedience which we owe to God, Who is the source of that authority, and against the charity and brotherly love which are due to our brethren.
(2) All are bound to uphold and assist the Government, which is lawfully constituted authority of the country and represents therefore, *in its own appointed sphere,* the authority of God Himself.[14]

Acquiescence on the part of the Catholic Social Guild was prompt despite the difficulty. In the succeeding issue of *The Christian Democrat* John B. Reeves commented:

To very many Catholics, and especially to members of the Catholic Social Guild, the condemnation of the recent strike by Cardinal Bourne came as a shock and an embarrassment. It found us in a state of excited tension which made calm reflection difficult, and obedience as painful as obedience can be, and must be sometimes if it is Christ-like. . . . The world is already acknowledging the wisdom of the Cardinal's pronouncement on the two grounds that appeal to it most: expedience and accepted law. The High Court has condemned the strike as illegal, and the strike-leaders have been as prompt as any to accept the verdict.[15]

---

14 Quoted in "The Challenge to Authority," *The Tablet,* CXLVII (May 15, 1926), 639.
15 "The National Crisis," VI (June, 1926), 91.

J. M. Cleary succinctly summarized the Catholic Social Guild's reaction to the Cardinal's intervention:

> *The Christian Democrat's* articles on this intervention went to press within a week of the collapse of the General Strike. They ranged from a searching analysis of the Cardinal's statement by a Dominican . . . to a severe denunciation of the strike by Henry Somerville, and these were followed in July by an eirenic article on Authority by a Benedictine. There were no more inquests.[16]

The demands of the miners at this time and the general strike met opposition from other Catholics. *The Tablet* voiced its opinion prior to the strike date: "If he [the miner] is determined to stand up against any reduction of wages, he must at least be willing to work a little longer and harder."[17] On the general strike *The Tablet* was in complete accord with Cardinal Bourne. Opposition to the continued miners' strike was based on alleged Russian financial aid to the miners.[18]

> To our minds the outstanding fact is that the miners' leaders have accepted over £250,000 from Russia, and that they announce their intention of continuing their struggle with the help of this money. During the General Strike Russia made it plain that she was offering help because of her firm conviction that the struggle in Great Britain was political rather than industrial . . . *The Tablet's* sympathy with the miners has often been expressed; but unless and until the avowed enemies of our institutions in Russia are repudiated as allies by the miners' organizations we and many other Britons must hold back our good will.[19]

The Month implied opposition to any strike on the part

---

16 *Op. cit.,* pp. 116–117.

17 "News and Notes," *The Tablet,* CXLVII (April 17, 1926), 525.

18 G. D. H. Cole states: "Headquarters refused, for tactical reasons, a subscription offered by the Russian Trade Union Council." *Op. cit.,* p. 490.

19 "News and Notes," *The Tablet,* CXLVII (May 22, 1926), 644.

of the miners, though it recognized that ". . . the miners are fighting for a just cause. . . ."[20] Prior to the April thirtieth walkout or lockout, commentary on the situation intimated disapproval of strike action:

> There should be no talk of a strike. The last foolish stoppage of work in 1921 cost the country £300,000,000 and helped to create the present uneconomic condition of industry. A strike would merely cripple industry at home and bring about the loss of foreign trade. The whole country would be further impoverished, and less able to offer assistance when negotiations were resumed. We cannot think that any responsible miners' leader has any thought of a strike.[21]

The same trend of thought is revealed in succeeding issues of *The Month*: "No one except the thoughtless wanted a strike: no one could expect any good from it proportionate to the cost."[22] And again: "The stoppage itself, coming when it did, after the costly eight months subsidy and the elaborate Report[23] which at least merited detailed consideration, was the acme of childish unwisdom, unworthy of grown-up men."[24] It is true that culpability for the strike was attributed also to Communist influence, to the ill-will of the owners, to mutual suspicion between the government and the Trades Union Congress, and to a lack of statesmanship; yet, support for the miners' case was meager.

The failure to arrive at an equitable settlement in 1926 presaged a continuance of the coal-industry problems. On the whole, the Social Catholic movement, and particularly the Catholic Social Guild, maintained its position of favoring the

---

[20] "Topics of the Month," *The Month*, CXLVIII (November, 1926), 457.

[21] *Ibid.*, CXLVII (May, 1926), 463.

[22] *Ibid.* (June, 1926), 549.

[23] Samuel Report, *supra*, p. 42, n.

[24] "Topics of the Month," *The Month*, CXLVIII (August, 1926), 176.

case of the miners and, when feasible, endorsing strike action. Pius XI's commemorative encyclical, *Quadragesimo Anno,* which appeared in 1931, encouraged pursuit of the policy. Writing in 1935, Patrick Bartley stated: "Nobody wishes to see a stoppage in the industry, though the miners can quite justly prefer a stoppage to the present unjust level of wages."[25] Strikes did occur, and they continued even after nationalization of the industry. They were generally unofficial,[26] local stoppages, occurring more frequently in some areas than in others. Wages, hours, working conditions persisted as the causes. Instigation of the strikes is difficult to ascertain and intensive research would be required to determine the exact role played by the Social Catholic movement in this regard.[27]

Nationalization: Departing from its established policy of setting forth general Catholic principles upon which social,

---

[25] "The Miner's Case," *The Christian Democrat,* XV (December, 1935) , 186.

[26] George B. Baldwin contends: "The absence of official strikes in recent years reflects the NUM feeling that the strike has become an outmoded means of getting what it wants. Arbitration is easier, cheaper, and almost as sure" (*Beyond Nationalization* [Cambridge, Massachusetts: Harvard University Press, 1955], p. 72).

[27] Baldwin has a pertinent footnote in his study: "There is a strong Irish Catholic element in Glasgow (the "Glasgow Irish" and the "Liverpool Irish" are well-known "types" in Britain). The Catholic Church, through an organization known as the Catholic Guild, is reported to have been more responsible than the Communists, for instance, in the numerous 1947 strikes for an increase for the lower-paid workers in Lanarkshire. On the Edinburgh side, in the Lothians, there is an organization known as Protestant Action, which has been active in local branches on that side of the coalfield. The rivalry between the Guild and Protestant Action was described as "bitter," but I did not get close enough to the industry in Scotland to get any firsthand evidence. After being told that some of the Catholic Guild leaders at the local level are also Communist Party members, one hesitates to come down hard with an opinion as to the relative roles of the Catholic Church and the Communist Party in the highly volatile Lanarkshire coalfield!" (*Op. cit.,* p. 80) .

economic, and political programs could be constructed, the Catholic Social Guild in 1921 took up the defense of, and the campaign for, the adoption of a specific proposed plan. Fundamentally the system was ". . . based upon the productivity not of districts but of the whole country. The more fortunately placed districts . . . would make some sacrifice, partly of profits but mainly of wages, in order to bring wages in the poorer districts to a higher level. This is the aim of what is called the National Pool."[28] Underlying the system were basic principles advocated by the Catholic Social Club, viz.:

1. The Living Wage has the first claim on the industry. . . .
2. If the industry as at present conducted cannot pay the living wage, there is a *prima facie* case for a change of system. . . .
3. . . . agreements to relate profits to wages. . . .
4. . . . no question of the owners' profits is a principal factor in the present deadlock. . . .
5. . . . Owners and miners should . . . regard themselves as partners in a national service. . . .[29]

Approval of the plan was also accorded by *The Tablet* because of it's "moral grounds." However, *The Tablet* entertained some doubt as to its practicability and stated:

The plan has, indeed, many difficulties of detail, and it has little chance of working successfully unless it is adopted with good will by all concerned. But because of its moral merits . . . and its potentialities as a basis of permanent industrial peace in the mining industry, we urge that it be given the best possible consideration by those who have the determination of the future organization of the industry in their hands.[30]

---

[28] "The Way to a Settlement," *The Christian Democrat,* I (June, 1921), 3.
[29] *Ibid.,* p. 4.
[30] "C.S.G. and the Coal Dispute," *The Tablet,* CXXXVIII (May 7, 1921), 602.

A peculiar objection, not to the plan itself but to the fact that the miners should offer a solution, was expressed by *The Month*: "If they could get their due otherwise, they were not justified in trying to force either nationalization or the pool on the other parties to the dispute. Such changes as these can only be made by national legislation, in which the community has a say."[31] Voicing further grievances against the miners, the article continues:

> After the failure of the desperate bid for the support of the railmen and transport workers on "Black Friday" (April 15th) the miners should have made terms. . . . We have often pointed out that, if the majority of the working classes believed in the programme of their leaders, they, having a preponderant vote in most constituencies, would surely return Labour men to Parliament. Instead of which they return Capitalists![32]

There was an apparent unanimity among Catholics in opposing the miner's request for the nationalizing of the mines[33] during the 1920's, though almost all recognized the need for some government control or amalgamation of some sort. With the new decade came a change in attitude. As early as January, 1931, G. K. Chesterton had declared himself in favor of na-

[31] "Topics of the Month," *The Month*, CXXXVIII (July, 1921), 76.

[32] *Ibid.*

[33] Many instances indicating the opposition might be cited; e.g.: "This is not to suggest nationalization of the coal industry; for commerce, we think, is not the business of the state, . ." ("Topics of the Month," *The Month,* CXXXVII [May, 1921], 459).

"The nationalization of the mines . . . is being put forward as a possible remedy. . . . At best, would not the nationalization of the mines be only the same state of things called by a different name?

"No matter what avenue you take towards your promised land through Nationalization, however broad and direct it may at first appear, it leads at last, if the policy be pursued upon a general scale, to the Servile State . . ." ("The Nationalization of the Mines," *Blackfriars,* VII [July, 1926], 395–396).

tionalization under certain conditions.[34] Two years later he stated specifically:

> . . . we have always allowed that some few matters are in their nature a national concern. The coal-mining industry is one of them. It is vital to our present economy, and it cannot be distributively organized to advantage. . . . we advocate national handling of the coal supply. . . .[35]

Gradually this change of opinion permeated society; seemingly the statement of Pius XI in *Quadragesimo Anno*—"It is rightly contended that certain forms of property must be reserved to the state, since they carry with them an opportunity of domination too great to be left to private individuals without injury to the community at large"[36]—was having its effect. Pius XII reiterated his predecessor's declaration at various times,[37] adding the stipulation of just compensation to the previous owners. The controversy which developed among Catholics in England as the nationalizing era approached was not whether nationalization as such was acceptable, but whether conditions in the particular instances warranted it.

Trade Unions. Labor organization problems were closely allied with the industrial conditions of 1920-1955. By the beginning of this period the "New Unionism"—industrial rather than craft unions—had been established. Its most salient tenet was worker control of industry. This idea, obscure and un-

---

[34] "Face the Facts," *G. K.'s Weekly*, XII (January 10, 1931), 277–278.

[35] "Many Manouvers," *G. K.'s Weekly*, XVIII (September 28, 1933), 50.

[36] Husslein, *op. cit.*, p. 220.

[37] For instance, radio address on the fifth anniversary of the outbreak of the war: "Who Are to be the Architects." *The Tablet*, CLXXXIV (September 9, 1944), 125; address to the First National Convention of Christian Association of Italian Workers in Rome: "Future of Trade Unions," *The Tablet*, CLXXXV (March 24, 1945), 138.

defined, was derived from a conglomeration of doctrinaire socialism, syndicalism, the theories of the Webbs, and guild socialism,[38] which was most influential in the war decade. By 1920 the labor force, with the greater number united by union affiliation in the Trades Union Congress, considered itself a power to be reckoned with, a power that could change the social order.[39] Optimistic in outlook, it viewed the shop

---

[38] Guild socialism was not clearly defined, but it was generally understood to embody the "Socialist doctrines of State ownership of capital and the elimination of the wage system. . . . Deriving its inspiration from two conflicting philosophies, Christian and Marxist, a compromise of this sort was bound to collapse." (G. W. F. "Some Modern Mediaevalists," *The Christian Democrat*, VI [August, 1926], 121–122). Edward J. Kiernan, in *Arthur J. Penty: His Contribution to Social Thought*, comments: "The Guild Socialist Movement . . . began as a *via media* between the aspirations of the State Socialists, with preponderant governmental regulation and bureaucracy and the claims of the Syndicalists, for whom the State counted nothing" (Washington, D.C.: Catholic University of America Press, 1941, p. 138). Georgiana Putnam McEntee declared: "In spite of efforts at clarification by its chief exponents, S. G. Hobson Orage, Penty and Cole, . . . the whole scheme remains too vague as to its general nature and too divergent in its details to be susceptible of clear exposition, . . . Certain features, however, stand out. It is neither Individualistic, nor Socialistic, though it has elements in common with the latter systems, and probably even more points of contact with theoretical Syndicalism. There is behind the movement a tacit assumption of the Marxian theory of value and an inspiration drawn from revolutionary trade unionism" (*The Social Catholic Movement in Great Britain* [New York: The Macmillian Company, 1927], p. 119). Concerning Labor's unwarranted demands in regard to "self-government in industry," Walter Milne-Bailey felt that guild socialism exercised some good influence: "The Guild Socialist movement did something to put these claims in their proper perspective, but there was still a good deal of muddle thinking on the subject" (*Trade Unions and the State* [London: George Allen and Unwin Ltd., 1934], p. 360).

[39] Alan Flanders, *Trade Unions* (New York: Hutchinson's University Library, 1952), p. 19.

steward movement[40] and Whitleyism[41] as milestones on the way to worker control. Dreams, hopes, and plans were soon shattered. The depression of 1920 was the introduction to a decade of reversals that left the unions numerically weakened and curtailed in activity, and the workers subjected to increased hours and lowered wages. Nevertheless, trade unionism rallied and channeled its energies into greater consolidation, the formation of a more definite economic policy, and political action to achieve its aims. While worker control of industry remained the dominant goal, it was now more clearly delineated, and the "conception of trade unionism as a willing and essential partner in the conduct of the nation's economic affairs steadily gained acceptance both within the movement and in society at large."[42] For a number of years political activity was circumscribed by the government to stay the growing power of the Labour party. The Act of 1927 required that a union member state in writing if he wished to pay the "political levy"—he had to "contract in." Prior to

---

[40] The shop steward was "popularly elected and officially recognized." His duties were to: "Look after his fellow-workers' interests generally. He is spokesman with the foreman, adjusts minor differences . . . and in general carries grievances or suggestions higher up. . . . As one of themselves he wields an immense influence that can often tip the scales between a peaceful settlement or a lightning strike" (Charles Pridgeon, S.J., *Opportunity for Trade Unionists* rev. ed. [Oxford: Catholic Social Guild, 1950], pp. 42–43) .

[41] In 1916 "the Government set up a sub-committee . . . under the chairmanship of Mr. J. H. Whitley, M.P., then Speaker of the House of Commons, to enquire into the causes of the trouble and to make recommendations 'for securing a permanent improvement in the relations between employers and workmen.' " The most important and most far-reaching report of the Whitley Committee was that dealing with conciliation and arbitration. The proposed system of Joint Industrial Councils was put into effect and continues to function in some areas even today. (Pridgeon, *op. cit.*, pp. 83–88.)

[42] Flanders, *op. cit.*, p. 23.

43

1927, and since 1945, the member paid the levy unless he stated his opposition in writing—he "contracts out."[43]

Through all the vicissitudes and adversities in the labor force development, the Social Catholic movement persisted in upholding the unions and their rights. "The Workers' Charter" of Leo XIII, issued thirty years prior to the period under consideration, had left doubt in no one's mind as to man's right of association, and it had outlined the fundamental principles upon which workers should base their organization in order to obtain social justice. But the encyclical also emphasized the need for class cooperation: "Each requires the other; capital cannot do without labour, nor labour without capital."[44] And more specifically:

> The rights and duties of employers, as compared with the rights and duties of the employed, should be made the subject of careful consideration. In case either a master or a workman deems himself injured, it will be most desirable to have in the organization a committee composed of honest and capable members whose duty it will be to decide the dispute according to the rules of the association.[45]

It was in the spirit of this teaching that the Social Catholic movement piloted its defense of trade unionism. As mentioned previously,[46] the Catholic Social Guild in 1921 proclaimed "Partnership Instead of Class Antagonism in Industry" as one of the planks in its platform. This continued to be the basis of its thought and writing to effect social justice for the worker and, in general, to obtain improved industrial and economic conditions.

---

[43] For a brief discussion see Adolph Fox Sturmthal, *Unity and Diversity in European Labor* (Glencoe, Illinois: The Free Press, 1953), pp. 41–43.

[44] Husslein, *op. cit.*, I, p. 177.

[45] *Ibid.*, p. 202.

[46] *Supra*, p. 30.

Thus, whatever was done toward improving worker-employer relations was highly commended. The Joint Industrial Councils plan inaugurated subsequent to the Whitley Reports was considered a step in the right direction. Though inherent weaknesses[47] rendered much of its attempted work nugatory, Charles Pridgeon, S.J., nevertheless, perceived beneficial consequences of the scheme:

> The net result of the Whitley investigation and its sequel can be summed up by saying that between the two wars relations between trade unions, employers' associations and the State have assumed a pattern in which a judicious blending of voluntary initiative with statutory legislation has made a notable contribution to industrial peace. Moreover, in this threefold partnership there is explicit testimony in the legislation and its administration that the cardinal principle of the State's intervention is to assist and promote the voluntary efforts of the other two, not to supersede them.[48]

The Mond-Turner[49] conference of 1928 was also accounted a landmark in the uphill struggle for understanding between the worker and his employer. In retrospective study of the discussions, Basil H. Tripp epitomized their significance:

---

[47] The chief of these is the council's lack of power to enforce agreements. For a further brief discussion see Mary Roddy, "The Whitley Councils Scheme," *The Christian Democrat,* XVIII (December, 1938), 185–186.

[48] *Op. cit.,* p. 88.

[49] "In 1927, Sir A. Mond [Lord Melchett] and a group of influential employers invited the Trades Union Congress to confer with them on a wide variety of questions relating to industrial reorganization and industrial relations. A series of conferences followed, and a number of agreed statements were issued dealing with a variety of topics" (Milne-Bailey, *op. cit.,* p. 147) . In 1930 a scheme of joint consultation and cooperation was agreed upon between the Trades Union Congress and the two national organizations of employers, the National Confederation of Employers' Organizations and the Federation of British Industries.

45

For the first time in our industrial history, capital and labour came together in an atmosphere uninfluenced by political considerations or prior engagements, and discussed their problems with unexampled frankness.

From the viewpoint of the trade-unionists, the Turner-Melchett conference and their outcome were of great importance and value. They served in a sense to codify the desires of organized labour, and in the eyes of the community as a whole they definitely established the claim of the unions to recognition as a permanent and vital part of the industrial structure. Whereas in former days trade-unionism felt itself anything but secure, and believed itself to be facing a hostile front at every point, the movement inaugurated by the late Lord Merchett established, beyond a shadow of a doubt, agreement upon its necessity and permanence.[50]

In the "Joint Pastoral Letter of the Hierarchy of England and Wales" issued in July, 1942, copartnership was included as one of the ten minimum conditions for a Christian way of life. It read: "Employers and employed should be regarded as partners not as rivals; they should unite to secure the best conditions for work, the fairest division of output, and the maximum of harmony."[51]

Various channels were employed to develop proper attitudes toward and understanding of labor unions and to develop intelligent leadership, based on Catholic social teaching, among both employees and employers. The study club was the principle means of instructing the workingman and imbuing him with Catholic social principles, and from its early days the study of trade unions was widespread. In 1924 the Lancashire Council of Study Clubs drew up the "Twelve Points for Catholic Trade Unionists," which was a

---

[50] "Co-partnership and Trade Unionism," *The Christian Democrat*, XV (February, 1935), 20–21.

[51] Quoted in Andrew Gordon, S.J., *Security, Freedom and Happiness* (Oxford: Samuel Walker, Ltd., 1948), p. 205.

plan for organized study.[52] In 1920 and in 1946 handbooks
for social study which included outlines for courses on trade
unionism were published by the Catholic Social Guild. The
1946 issue was "reprinted five times, twice revised, and
appeared in a new edition in 1953."[53] In 1948 Charles Pridgeon's *Opportunity for Trade Unionists* was published as a
textbook. Perennial favorites for study club discussion were
Rerum Novarum and *Quadragesimo Anno,* which provided
worker and employer with pertinent material. Though the
study club had begun, and had reached unforeseen success,
among the workingmen, it proved advantageous in propagating Catholic social principles and in ameliorating social and
economic relationships among other groups as well. J. M.
Cleary states that in 1947 "The study-clubs ranged from
groups of university students and teachers in training, through
seminary groups and sections of the Knights of St. Columbus
and C.Y.M.S. to the primordial groups of interested workers. . . ."[54]

Catholic Social Guild publications on trade unionism and
worker-employer relations, exclusively or inclusively, for the
general reading public constituted a considerable list; for
example:

1929 *A Code of Social Principles*
1930 *Trade Unions and Employers' Associations; the
Catholic View.* A Letter from the Sacred Congre-
gation of the Council to the Bishop of Lille.
1946 *Light and Life for Trade Unionists*
1947 *Counter Attack in the Unions,* by Robert P. Walsh
1949 *The Christian Workingman*
1951 *Fresh Deal for Management and Labour,* by Robert
W. Johnson

---

[52] Cleary, *op. cit.,* p. 90.
[53] *Ibid.,* p. 194, n. The 1923 handbook substituted a course on
Guild Socialism for that on trade unionism.
[54] *Ibid.,* p. 195.

47

1954 *Human Relations in Industry,* by Michael P. Fogarty
1956 *The Social Teaching of Pius XII,* by Cyril C.
Clump, S.J.[55]

In addition, relevant articles appeared regularly in the monthly issues of *The Christian Democrat.*

The Catholic Workers' College aimed from its foundation in 1921 to prepare workers for leadership among their own people, fulfilling the statement of Pope Pius XI in *Quadragesimo Anno*: ". . . the first and immediate apostles of the workingmen must themselves be workingmen."[56] From its inception the course "History, Theory and Practice of Trade Unions" was offered. In 1952 ex-students of the College were in office in trade unions, while many others were influential as regular members.[57]

---

[55] *Ibid., passim.*

[56] Husslein, *op. cit.,* p. 231.

[57] Cleary, *op. cit.,* p. 152. The activity of Ted Colgan, a student in the early 1920's, illustrates the tremendous opportunities of penetrating society and spreading Catholic social teaching open to a trained workman: "Edward Colgan returned to the mines and completed fifty-three years underground. Lodge Chairman. Chairman of North-East Federation of Trades Councils. First National Chairman of Association of Catholic Trades Unionists. Stood for Urban District Council 1927, 1930, unsuccessfully. County Councillor for Blaydon East, 1946. Chairman of County Planning Committee of Tyneside River Board. Vice-Chairman of northern region of the Housing and Town Planning Association. Member of the Board of Governors of the United Newcastle-on-Tyne Teaching Hospital since 1948. Chairman of Management Committee of Prudhoe and Monkton Mental Hospital, 1955. Chairman of Northern Tuberculosis After-Care Committee. Election agent, 1926–59. Executive member of the Constituency Labour Party. Recruited for R.A.F., 1930–45. Q.M.S., Home Guard. Chairman of local area committee of Ministry of Information. Conducted study-clubs and W.E.A. classes, 1926–1950. For twenty-five years secretary of the Tyneside Branch of the Guild. Member of the Society of St. Vincent de Paul. Grand Knight, Knights of St. Columba. Chairman of Executive Committee of C.S.G., Tyneside. Joint-founder (with Martin Brennan, a college

A third educational program through which labor and management were brought together was the Catholic Social Guild Summer School, which was conducted annually for one week. Lectures were frequently devoted to trade unionism, copartnership, and social topics bearing on employee-employer relations. But the greatest asset was the informal discussion in which both groups frankly participated. Reports of the summer schools systematically referred to this aspect:

> Dr. Fenelon's subject was Industrial Administration Today, and he dealt with such theory as hours of work, industrial fatigue, absenteeism, dilution of labour, training of women for munitions work, labour management, flow of production, etc. Some straight hitting, from the sides both of Management and Labour, followed this exposition: each side learnt the other's view-point—always a useful feature of the Summer School.[58]

And:

> The 175 men and women who came to the School to discuss "Industrial Democracy" were drawn from every class and station in life. Thereby their presence together bore miniature witness to the kind of society which is their industrial ideal. So, too, did their ability to mix. Where else, perhaps, but at a C.S.G. Summer School does one find an industrial manager caught up in a prolonged discussion with an eager group of trade unionists or good-humoredly seated after supper in the midst of a wider circle allowing himself to be "shot at" by all and sundry? This school was packed full of informal discussion, and that fact, perhaps, is the best tribute one can pay to the enthusiasm of its members.[59]

student 1928) of A.C.T.U. Presented with T.U.C. gold medal for long and distinguished service to the Trade Union Movement" (pp. 137–138).

[58] "The 1941 Summer School," *The Christian Democrat*, XXI (September, 1941), 140.

[59] Paul Crane, S.J., "The Catholic Social Guild Summer School," *The Tablet*, CC (August 16, 1952), 138.

In 1942 a new organization intended as a means of enabling the Catholic worker to be an influence for good in his union was launched as a part of the Social Catholic movement. This was the A.C.T.U.—Association of Catholic Trade Unionists. The English trade unions claimed a Christian tradition.[60] Basically they were in accord with Catholic social principles, having as aims and purposes, as Charles Pridgeon, S.J., pointed out:

> *Justice* or fair wages under good conditions of work, *Efficiency* or pride of craft and workmanship coupled with full production in quantity and quality at just prices in service to the community, *Order* or fair competition without sweating, *Brotherhood* or benevolent funds in various forms of insurance against unemployment, sickness, accident, retirement, death, and *Freedom* or protection against possible abuses at the hands of employers or the State.[61]

Nevertheless, anti-Christian forces were continuously at work and at times exercised undue influence upon the labor movement, undermining its Christian basis. The Social Catholic movement recognized the need for counteraction from within the unions;[62] hence, the formation of the Association of Catholic Trade Unionists.

At the Trades Union Congress at Blackpool in 1942 the immediate cause for the organization and concentration of effort on the part of Catholic trade unionists arose. A memorandum on education accepted by the Trades Union Congress

. . . proposed that in future any denomination wishing to

---

[60] Joseph Clayton traces the tradition in "Christian Tradition in the English Labour Movement," *Blackfriars,* XIX (April, 1938), 244–249.

[61] *Op. cit.,* p. 154.

[62] To have formed a separate Catholic union would only have given the anti-Christian forces free play in the existing unions. A Catholic union could be only an impotent, weak minority group. The idea was consistently opposed by leading English Catholics.

teach Religion in schools should build and maintain such schools itself. In effect the trade union movement, counting thousands of Catholics among its loyal members, was being used to press the Government into framing an Education Act which denied freedom of religion. Catholics could contract-out but, if they did, they were to be penalized with an impossible financial burden.[63]

Catholics were aroused by this denial of freedom of religion, and perceived as its source the Communist infiltration of the unions. A group of them, led by two former students at the Catholic Workers' College, Ted Colgan and Martin Brennan, with the approval of the Bishop of Hexham and Newcastle, formed the Diocesan Association of Catholic Trade Unionists. Through steady pressure and with the assistance of other Catholic organizations, it was effective in having the unjust educational proposal withdrawn. In the meantime, the idea of association "caught fire" and new groups were formed in parishes, deaneries, the towns, always with diocesan approval. By March, 1948, about twenty associations were in existence, and in October of 1947 a liaison committee was set up at a Manchester meeting to coordinate their work.[64] The association was not limited to trade unions. An item in *The Tablet*, June 18, 1949, announced the formation of a unit for "Catholics in Unions, Guilds or Associations of Professional Workers." It invited "all eligible, lawyers, doctors, journalists, scientific workers, Civil Servants, Bank and Insurance officials, etc.,"[65] to become members.

In general the association was to meet two needs: (1) to

---

[63] Pridgeon, *op. cit.*, p. 152. The author explains in a footnote that "The procedure by which the Memorandum was presented to Congress was a mockery of democratic method. It had never been placed before affiliated unions for previous discussion or consideration by them and their branch organizations" (*Ibid.*).

[64] Robert P. Walsh, "The British A.C.T.U.," *The Social Justice Review*, XL (March, 1948), 372.

[65] CXCIII, 405.

organize reaction to Communist intrigue; (2) to help Catholic trade unionists to be good Catholics and good trade unionists. Members required training in order to work effectively. A suggested preparatory plan was outlined by Robert P. Walsh:

(1) Regular retreats and days of recollection . . . as a help towards the full living of Faith. Further developments must bring in the Church's liturgy. . . .
(2) A knowledge of the Church's doctrine with special emphasis on her social teaching, to be secured by lectures, study circles, of C.T.S., C.S.G. and other suitable literature. . . .
(3) The work of an A.C.T.U. should be planned to emphasize opportunities for the members to speak and to take an active part in discovering the social teaching of the Church. A special watch should be kept for members displaying the particular qualities that would fit them for particular positions. Such members should receive special training and encouragement.
(4) The training should include practical tasks . . . doing little jobs that will take them more and more into the life of their union. . . .[66]

A discussion[67] on the achievements of the A.C.T.U. within approximately five years indicates that it exerted a considerable influence. Concerning "an election for a general secretaryship of a major union a well-known leader remarked that . . . he would not forecast this time because of the Catholics." For the first time in many years, the Communist domination of the London Trades Council was challenged by a group of Catholic delegates. A trades council meeting in a Lancashire town held "a long discussion on the Christian way to defeat

[66] "Counter Attack in the Unions," *Catholic Social Guild Leaflet*, No. 16 (Oxford: 1947), n. p.
[67] Robert P. Walsh, "The British A.C.T.U.," *The Social Justice Review*, XL (March, 1948), 372. Succeeding quotations and examples are taken from this article.

fascism." The overthrow of the Communist domination of the Executive Committee of the Civil Servants Clerical Association was a major achievement led by the secretary of Westminster A.C.T.U. Another "major achievement has been . . . that the Catholic vote has to be taken into account in the nation-wide union election." In one instance the Communist Party refrained from putting up a Communist candidate. In 1946 "of major officials of the four branches of the Amalgamated Engineering Union serving Ford workers there were about twenty (out of 24) communists. . . . Today there is only one and he will be rejected at the 1948 branch elections." Four years later Bishop George A. Beck stated: "Catholic trade unionists are today in key positions with the eyes of the Church upon them."[68]

Examples of the good accomplished by the A.C.T.U. might be multiplied. Yet, in 1946 Colm Brogan deplored the apathy of Catholic Trade Unionists: "Why is it that [their] very considerable numbers apparently count for nothing when there is voting on political resolutions, while the smaller number of Communists counts for so much?"[69] The writer advocated concentration "on giving an intensive education and formation to a selected body of intelligent workers who have energy and moral courage," and also the establishment of "an institute of Catholic studies in every large industrial town, where Catholic workers could be trained to do something more fruitful and effective than countering snippets from Communist pamphlets with snippets from Rerum Novarum."[70] Enthusiasm, energy, and influence of the Catholic trade unionists apparently did wane in the 1950's, and extensive Communist

[68] "The Opportunity Before the C.S.G.," *The Christian Democrat*, n.s., III (October, 1952), 225.

[69] "The T.U. and Their Catholic Members," *The Tablet*, CLXXXVIII (November 2, 1946), 227.

[70] *Ibid.*

infiltration again was evident. Literature of the Social Catholic movement again took on the plea for alert, intelligent Catholic trade unionist activity. The obvious need for it was evinced by such action as that of the Durham County Council on November 28, 1950, when "by an overwhelming majority the Socialist members carried a resolution and re-affirmed the Council's decision to apply a 'closed shop' for its employees."[71]

During the years 1920–1955 significant changes took place with regard to the power and strength of the trade unions, to their recognized place in the political realm as well as in the social and economic realms, and to the extent of profit sharing, copartnership, and worker control. Generally, the Social Catholic movement supported the aims and goals of the workers, but it was careful, too, to observe the directions of the Holy See. At the October, 1953, meeting of the International Union of Social Studies a group devoted its investigation to a declaration on workers' control in a firm. The body of papal directives on the subject was found to contain three kinds of statements: affirmative, negative, and neutral; e.g., *Quadragesimo Anno*:

> . . . We deem it advisable that the wage contract should, when possible, be modified somewhat by a contract of partnership. . . . In this way workers and officials are made sharers in the ownership or the management, or in some way participate in the profits.[72]

Pius XII, radio message to Spanish workers, March 11, 1951:

> The Church sees with satisfaction and encourages moves—circumstances permitting—to introduce elements of partnership into the wage contract.[73]

---

[71] Charles Pridgeon, S.J., "Death Blow to Trade Unions," *The Christian Democrat*, new ser., II (January, 1951), 3.

[72] Husslein, *op. cit.*, p. 202.

[73] Quoted in Malines Union, "Workers Control," *The Christian Democrat*, new ser., V (March, 1954), 168.

Pius XII, allocution of June 3, 1950:

> Neither the nature of the wage-contract nor that of the firm is such as necessarily and of itself to imply a right to joint control of commercial decisions.[74]

Pius XII, letter to Turin Social Week, 1952:

> Workers have in principle no strict right to a share in control. But there is nothing to stop employers offering their workers an appropriate type and degree of shared control.[75]

Similar statements carrying the social doctrine to the present day have been made by Pope John XXIII in *Mater et Magistra,* e.g.:

> . . . We defend the desire of employees to participate actively in the management of enterprises in which they are employed.[76]

The Malines union declaration observed, on the one hand, that employers should not behave as autocrats, nor should they have too little confidence in the personal abilities of their workers; and, on the other hand, that workers must free themselves from suspicions and class war mentality, and must recognize their duties and obligations as well as their rights. It was this last point that Father Paul Crane, S.J., had in mind when he wrote:

> . . . it is possible for capital and labour, for trade unions and management . . . to have the best of relations and to look after each other's interests to the full whilst continuing at the same time to exploit the consumer. An improvement in industrial relations need not be accompanied by increased productivity. Higher wages can be bought at the expense of the consumer. That . . . is the case today . . . in industry as a whole and, so long as it

---

[74] *Ibid.,* 169.
[75] *Ibid.,* 170.
[76] (New York: The America Press, 1961), p. 26.

remains so, the best long-run interests . . . of the whole country remains in jeopardy.[77]

Thus, while the Social Catholic movement approved the labor movement in general, it did not hesitate to censure and decry injustice and overriding ambition on the part of the trade unions. It adhered to its policy of disseminating Catholic social principles—praise or blame was incidental.

Guild Social Order. Because of this policy, and because of its conviction of the necessity for a "reconstruction of the social order," the Social Catholic movement committed itself to explaining and advocating the Guild Social Order, sketchily outlined but highly recommended, by Pope Pius XI in *Quadragesimo Anno.* Basic to the plan is the principle of subsidiarity. The Guilds of Vocational Groups were to be initiated, not by the state, nor by the Church, nor by any other dominating authority but by the workers, managers, and employers themselves. Hence, the vital necessity of thoroughly indoctrinating Catholics, and others also, with the principles and essence of the scheme, and also of indicating a practical application for England.

Extensive writing was done on the subject through the 1930's, particularly in the pages of *The Christian Democrat* and in books published by the Catholic Social Guild. The *Catholic Social Year Book, 1936* was entitled "The Guild Social Order" and comprised a series of essays which represented comprehensive thought and study of the matter. The range of topics included "Industrial Relations and the Duty of the State," "The Development of the Guild Social Order," "The Place of Trade Unions in the Guild System," "Towards a Guild Order in Great Britain," and "Corporative Organization." While the writers appreciated the great merits

---

[77] "Beside the Point," *The Christian Democrat,* new ser., IV August, 1953), 170.

of the system, they were also aware of the problems involved in establishing the Guild Social Order. Difficulties presented themselves chiefly in relationship to the state—". . . the twin dangers of being swallowed by the State or of swallowing the State. . . ."[78]—and to the existing trade unions—"The Guild looks at realities from the viewpoint of production, wealth and economic efficiency. . . . Trade unionism. . . . looks at realities from the viewpoint of social conditions and human rights."[79]

The idea of the Guild Social Order did not attain popularity, and consequently its benefits were not experienced in England. There were some who felt that the prevailing English system approached the papal scheme. Charles Pridgeon, S.J., pointed out a possible affinity:

> In Great Britain Whitleyism comes near to a working model of this hierarchical organization. A strong tradition of liberty has assured to us associations that are free and not mere appendages of the State. Trade unions, employers' associations and professional bodies are groups each with their own interests and common aims. Joint Industrial Councils and the proposed Development Councils are a wider instance of the same principle based on the common interests of both sides in the trade or industry and their essential link with the wider interests of the community. . . . Their point is that they stand for co-operation in the making and in the sharing of the product with an eye on the common good of the nation, and offer the natural and obvious alternative to war between the so-called haves and have-nots.[80]

Bishop George A. Beck viewed the situation very differently:

[78] E. Delaye, "The Guild Principle—Some Critical Points," *The Christian Democrat*, XIX (June, 1939), 92.

[79] *Ibid.* (July, 1939), 104. The author gives a penetrating discussion of the difficulties in an article published serially in the May to September issues.

[80] *Op. cit.*, p. 94.

Certainly there is a vast gap between the trade-union attitude in this country today and Papal ideal of vocational groups. On the one hand, as I see it, is the perpetuation of the conflict between Capital and Labour; on the other, there is the growing desire to extend State authority over industry—and both these ideas are diametrically opposed to the Papal plan of *self-governing vocational groups*.[81]

In the opinion of the bishop, however, corporatism or the Guild Social Order was the solution to the social and economic problems, and it would be brought about "in the measure in which Catholic ideas are disseminated throughout it [the trade union movement] by Catholic trade unionists."[82]

Political Parties. Almost inevitably and inextricably the labor movement in England was linked with politics because of its ties with Labour party. Though not obligated, the overwhelming majority of workers claimed membership in the Labour party; affiliation with the Conservative and Liberal parties during the period under consideration was limited. In the aggregate, Catholics were generally numbered in the working class; hence, they were predominantly Labour party members. Unfortunately, the Labour party had been labeled as socialistic, which, as such—if it embodied antireligious tenets—would ban Catholics from membership, in accord with the papal condemnation of socialism.

The Social Catholic movement had no part in politics, but it operated on the bases so well stated for Catholic action, viz., that it concerned itself with politics:

(i) indirectly, by forming consciences and diffusing the Christian social principles which are to orientate all manifestations of public life;

[81] "The Opportunity Before the C.S.G.," *The Christian Democrat,* new ser., III (October, 1952), 223–224.
[82] *Ibid.,* 225.

(ii) directly, when politics touch on morality or religion.[83]

Practically, it attempted to resolve the conflict concerning
the socialism attributed to the Labour party, and pointed out
the rights and duties of the state and of the citizens.

In 1918 the Labour party adopted a constitution, a clause
of which embodied an ownership tenet very like that of
Continental socialism. The controversy over Catholic membership raged anew. Cardinal Bourne, cognizant of the
dilemma created for Catholics, issued the statement ". . . that
the way to judge the Labour Party was by what it did and
not by what it said in a Constitution."[84] Repeatedly Cardinal
Bourne insisted that English Catholics were free to join any
of the major political parties: ". . . a Catholic man or woman
may be a zealous worker for Conservatism or for Labour
or for Liberalism without the slightest infidelity to the
Church."[85] And ". . . as at present no political party in this
country was openly opposed to Catholic principles, Catholics
might therefore belong to any party they chose."[86] In 1931
the Cardinal declared that the condemnation of socialism by
Pius XI in *Quadragesimo Anno* did not apply to the English
Labour party. "The reason for this exception is that English
Socialism is purely pragmatic, contrary to that of the Continent, and it is entirely neutral on the philosophical and
religious level."[87] This viewpoint was corroborated by Car-

---

[83] Luigi Civardi, *A Manual of Catholic Action,* trans. C. C. Martindale, S.J. (New York: Sheed & Ward, Inc., 1936), p. 193.

[84] Robert P. Walsh, "Catholics in the Labour Party," *The Christian Democrat,* new ser., VI (April, 1955), 197.

[85] "Catholics and Politics," *The Tablet,* CXLV (January 17,
1925), 67.

[86] "An East End Catholic Rally," *Ibid.,* 74.

[87] Daniel O'Connor, *Catholic Social Doctrine* (Westminster, Maryland: The Newman Press, 1956), p. 76.

dinal Bourne's successors, Cardinal Hinsley and Cardinal Griffin, who also declared that "English Catholics are free to join the British Labor Party."[88]

Despite these authoritative assertions of the English hierarchy, there were individuals, able to command some following, who saw the Labour party only as following the line of doctrinaire socialism.[89] Their consideration of, and efforts at establishing, a Catholic party were consistently deprecated by the leaders of the Church in England. Cardinal Bourne objected, not only because he considered a Catholic political party impractical ". . . but also because the profession of the Catholic Faith did not imply a common outlook in political affairs. . . ."[90] The Catholic Social Guild was in agreement with the hierarchy on English socialism and Catholic political parties, and *The Christian Democrat* systematically sustained these opinions.

At all times Catholics were urged by the Social Catholic movement to participate in political affairs—not only in the sense of fulfilling their duty in the exercise of the right of franchise but also in running for office, locally and nationally. Comparatively, Catholics were poorly represented at all levels,

---

[88] Raymond J. Miller, *Forty Years After: Pius XI and the Social Order* (St. Paul, Minnesota: Radio Replies Press, 1947), p. 252.

[89] Two occasions may be cited: (1) Following the Labor Party's adoption of the new constitution, Thomas F. Burns, Secretary of the National Confederation of Catholic Trade Unionists, led a group of workers in the attempt to establish the Centre Labour Party. He contended it was not a "confessional" party, but it took on the aspects of such. (2) Hamish Fraser, writing in *The Christian Democrat,* VI (April, 1955), 199–208, provoked controversy by his contention that Catholics could not belong to any British political party because basically they were all "Socialist in the sense that their doctrine 'conceives human society in a way utterly alien to Christian truth.'"

[90] "Notes and Comments," *The Christian Democrat,* XV (February, 1935), 1.

and especially in the House of Commons, where the Labour party was the party with the largest Catholic membership.[91] While Catholic officials and representatives would maintain and act on Catholic principles, they were to ". . . vote and speak as good citizens . . . labouring for the general good."[92] Cardinal Bourne ". . . rejoiced in the number of Catholics in Parliament, less because their presence would further Catholic interests than because it was a manifestation of the concern of Catholics as citizens with the affairs of their country."[93] Cardinal Griffin, addressing the Catholic Parents' and Electors' Association at Brighton in 1948, again emphasized the obligation of Catholics to vote and, that being done, "to see what legislation is being passed through Parliament, and to make known [their] views to the candidate who represents [them]."[94] He urged his audience to join a political party and to become active within it. The need for Catholics in government positions—Catholics aware of their duties, fully informed on Catholic social principles—to influence legislation concerning such fundamental questions as education, divorce, and birth control became ever greater. A conference for Catholic councillors, meeting under the auspices of the Interdiocesan Council of the Catholic Parents' and Electors' Associations and the Catholic Education Council in November, 1955, concluded on the conviction that

> not only is there even more need for Catholics to enter Local Government and other branches of public life, but that they must be properly prepared and kept fully in-

---

[91] "Notes and Comments," *The Christian Democrat*, IV (February, 1924) , 20.

[92] "Catholics in Public Life," *The Tablet*, CXLVIII (September 18, 1926) , 361.

[93] "Notes and Comments," *The Christian Democrat*, XV (February, 1935), 1.

[94] "Catholics in Public Life," *The Tablet*, CXCII (November 27, 1948) , 349.

formed, and above all, inspired with the ideal of service to their fellow countrymen, in and through the political parties which they join.[95]

Just as the Social Catholic movement sought to leaven society with Catholic social principles by working from within, so, too, it advocated that Catholics work from within political parties to guide the government along Christian lines. Cardinal Griffin understood the necessity for such procedure and was not prone to exonerate the Catholic political apathy. His concluding remarks of an address, referred to previously, indicate his intolerance of the prevailing attitude: "To refrain from joining a party on the grounds that politics are sordid affairs is no excuse. It is sheer laziness."[96]

Fascism

The interwar years saw another political development which had repercussions among the English Catholics. It was the Fascist movement. Almost from its incipience in Italy it won the acclaim of the majority of the Catholics in England. Foremost in voicing approval was *The Tablet.* For approximately two decades it stood staunchly by *Il Duce,* excusing, explaining, defending, and lauding words and deeds of the Fascisti and their leader. There was no apparent comprehension of the basic tenets of Fascism, no awareness that Fascism had assumed nationalist elements and that "in religious policy the ideas of Rocco and Federzoni guided the rising *Duce* as he made his peace with much of old Italy, including the Catholic hierarchy."[97] Issue upon issue of *The Tablet* testi-

[95] "Catholics in Local Government," *The Tablet,* CCVI (November 12, 1955), 490.

[96] "Catholics in Public Life," *The Tablet,* CXCII (November 27, 1948), 349.

[97] Richard A. Webster, *The Cross and the Fasces* (Stanford, California: Stanford University Press, 1960), p. 197, n. 20.

In a pamphlet published in 1914 Alfredo Rocco, a Nationalist lawyer, elucidated the place of the Church in its role as a tool of

fies to its unqualified approval of Italian Fascism. Summary statements will illustrate:

> . . . the tone of much Osservatore comment in recent months has indeed given occasion for honest, thoughtful Fascists to feel aggrieved. No one can deny—the Pope himself has borne witness to it—the wonderfully good things which the present Government has done in matters appertaining to religion. . . . To say that "it is not wise to look a gift horse in the mouth" suggests the possibility that Fascism might go back on its religious dispositions, which it is not going to do.[98]

Signor Mussolini regards Italy as a Catholic nation, and his Fascismo, while reviving some ancient Roman customs, does not include a pagan reaction or any other kind of anti-Christian movement in its programme. As for the Papacy, the Duce is so fully convinced of its importance

---

the state: "The State should take into direct consideration the interests of Italian Catholics, insofar as they are compatible with the interests of the Nation. . . . The Nationalists believe that the State must assert its sovereignty also in regard to the Church. Since, however, they recognize that the Catholic religion and Church are most important factors of national life, they wish to watch over Catholic interests as far as possible, always safeguarding the sovereignty of the State. And at this stage of Italian life, such protection should take the form of respect for the freedom of conscience of Italian Catholics. . . . In the future it will perhaps be possible to go farther and establish an agreement with the Catholic Church, even if only tacit, by which the Catholic organization could serve the Italian nation for its expansion in the world" (quoted in Webster, *op. cit.,* p. 37) . It is noteworthy that in 1929 Rocco was the chief Fascist negotiator for the Lateran Pacts. Luigi Federzoni was one of the five Nationalist editors of *L'Idea Nazionale,* through which in 1912–1914 were made "the first real contacts between Nationalist Party spokesmen and the official organizations of Italian Catholicism. . . . Federzoni . . . did well under Fascism, but voted against Mussolini in the Grand Council of Fascism at the last fatal session of July 24, 1943" (*Ibid.,* p. 34) . In 1924 Federzoni was appointed Minister of the Interior by Mussolini.

[98] "Fascism and Religion," *The Tablet,* CXLVII (January 23, 1926), 120.

to Italy that the Roman Question is assuming a new orientation; . . . Catholics have had abundant cause for gratitude to Signor Mussolini. The sacred emblem of the Cross has been restored to historic buildings . . . Eastertide this year was rung in by the bell of the Capitol. Crucifixes have been brought back into schools and institutions . . . and Mass has been celebrated on many a long-abandoned altar. . . . But we do sympathize with those true friends of liberty who say that Fascismo has passed out of the martial law stage, and that its future stability will depend upon its inflexible justice. It is as well-wishers and sincere admirers of Signor Mussolini that we make these remarks.[99]

In his allocution at the Christmas Consistory in 1926 the Holy Father protested the continued, violent Fascist attacks upon Catholics individually and the "compulsory absorption of Catholic Youths' Associations, Boy Scouts, etc., by the National Fascist Balills organization. . . ."[100] With lucidity and insight he indicated the Fascist corporative state idea "which cannot be Catholic since all-absorbing and monopolizing, it makes the State the end and the Citizen, the Man but the instrument only therein."[101] Notwithstanding these deprecations, *The Tablet* maintained its position in favor of Fascist policy whether domestic or foreign, and on occasion expressed only "regret that our task should be made harder by what looks like unchivalrous and swaggering behaviour towards a State [Austria in this reference] too weak for reprisals."[102]

[99] "News and Notes," *The Tablet,* CXLVII (April 17, 1926), 526–527.

[100] M. Mansfield, "The Church and the Hour of Fascism," *The Dublin Review,* CLXXXI (July, 1927), 65.

[101] *Ibid.*

[102] "News and Notes," *The Tablet,* CL (March 10, 1928), 307. The situation concerned the Austrian complaint of mistreatment of the German-speaking Italian subjects. Mussolini threatened reprisals including the suppression of German-language newspapers and the dismissal of about a thousand German-speaking officials in the province involved.

Admiration was the keynote of all *The Tablet* carried concerning Mussolini and Italian Fascism, even to the point of deprecating English policies:

Il Duce has a Totalitarian mind which brings him into bruising collisions with a world run on piecemeal compromises. He ardently desired a Lausanne Conference which would deal with big problems in a big way. With clearer eyes than those British publicists whose precipitate optimism *The Tablet* deplored on the morrow of the Premier's return from Switzerland, Signor Mussolini perceives that the Lausanne Settlement is precariously contingent upon uncertain factors; . . .[103]

The economic and social accomplishments of the regime were perceived as an unequivocal benediction and were hailed as the great comfort for the amnestied political exiles returning in 1932:

They will see more trees on the hill-sides, more wheatfields in the vales; less disease, less misery and much less dirt. Fascist energy has wrought wonders in Italy. . . . We do not say that grandiose feats of material progress are everything. . . . In Italy's case ideals abound; and they are becoming less and less incompatible with the Catholic ethos. Totalitarianism's arrogant crest has been lowered; and it is a Catholic, as well as an old Roman force which has supplanted the bad old Masonic Italian-

---

[103] "News and Notes," *The Tablet*, CLX (July 23, 1932), 102. "The Lausanne Conference of June–July 1932 was held to liquidate the payment of reparations by Germany to the former Allied and Associated powers. Attended by representatives of the creditor powers (Great Britain, France, Belgium and Italy) and of Germany, the conference resulted in agreement on July 9, 1932, that the conditions of world economic crisis made continued reparation payments impossible. . . . The creditor governments canceled war debts as between themselves, but made a 'gentleman's agreement' about their own war debts to the United States. Although never ratified the Lausanne protocol in effect ended attempts to exact reparations from Germany" ("Lausanne Conferences," *Encyclopedia Britannica,* 1960 ed., Vol. XIII, p. 773).

ism of fifty years after 1870. Fascismo enters upon its second decade amidst more hopes than fears.[104]

Cardinal Hinsley, in a speech given at the Birmingham Catholic Re-union early in 1939, attested to the true position of the Church regarding Fascism:

> Fascism as a philosophy expounded by Mussolini himself is fundamentally as wrong as Communism or Nazism, because in the Duce's own words, which I quote, "Everything in the State; everything for the State; nothing outside the State." This means surely that the Church, the persons and the family are at the mercy of a party calling itself the State.
>
> .   .   .   .
>
> He [a Catholic] cannot adopt the ideology of the pagan State which the founders of Fascism proclaimed; viz., out and out totalitarianism. If he labels himself a Fascist in this country he is unwise and is not consulting the safety of the Catholic cause in England. He is . . . giving the impression that the Catholic Church is backing Fascism.[105]

Even so trenchant a statement from the highest Catholic authority in England apparently did not convince *The Tablet* of its error. As late as November, 1940, when the full significance of Italian Fascism stood unmasked before most of the world, *The Tablet* was still "grasping at straws"—referring to alleged policies of the past, and imputing interpretations to defend Fascism. The anti-Communist policy was extolled, for "Mussolini never flirted with Soviet ideology until the Axis compelled him to walk with Hitler. . . ."[106] When others pointed out that "Soviet Moscow and Fascist Rome have something in common,"[107] *The Tablet* naively commented:

---

[104] "Fascismo's Second Decade," *The Tablet,* CLX (October 29, 1932), 562.

[105] Quoted in "Notes and Comments," *The Christian Democrat,* XIX (May, 1939), 65.

[106] "A Fascist Twist," *The Tablet,* CLXXVI (November 2, 1940), 342.

[107] *Ibid.*

"We imagine these things are written as an indication to the Vatican that Fascism, being dynamic, could develop in any direction, and, if not better appreciated as a civilizing force at home, could seek admiration abroad."[108] "Or," said *The Tablet*, "these things may also be written as a hint for the Spaniards, that they would do much better to help break the blockade, and not, by standing aside, drive the Italians, and the Germans to the most desperate courses."[109]

While *The Tablet* was championing the cause of Italian Fascism, it was at the same time denouncing English Fascism under the leadership of Sir Oswald Mosley. It was no correlation between Continental Fascism and that of England. The Italian leader was esteemed, but according to *The Tablet*, "Sir Oswald Mosley is incalculably below Signor Mussolini in personal force and constructive ability. . . ."[110] "Gangsterism," which was excused and defended on the part of Italian Fascists, was condemned under all circumstances when involved in English Fascism. Whatever form Italy's Fascist politics followed was lauded, but the same tactics under Sir Oswald Mosley were intolerable. When Father Vincent McNabb, O.P., quoted a few of Mussolini's dictums, the editor of *The Tablet* queried: "Have they been punctiliously translated and has full justice been done to their context?"[111]

The persistence of *The Tablet* in its attitude toward Italian Fascism generally did not find a counterpart in the contemporary Catholic periodicals. However, the pro and con articles carried portrayed an indecisive policy, and revealed the tendency of English Catholics, on the whole, to favor it. Thus, *The Dublin Review* printed such opinions as:

---

108 *Ibid.*, 343.

109 *Ibid.*

110 "News and Notes," *The Tablet*, CLXIII (June 23, 1934) , 78.

111 "Letters to the Editor," *The Tablet*, CLXIII (June 23, 1934) , 800. Volumes of *The Tablet* in the early 1930's abound in criticism of Sir Oswald Mosley and his British Fascist Union, while the same volumes, and others, approve of Mussolini and his Italian Fascism.

Fascism has come to realize that on religion the inmost and deepest life of a nation rests; . . . It is God's purpose that mankind be engaged upon earth in a ceaseless mission, and it is in this spirit that the new Italy, in proportion as she is being moulded by the forces which every day grow stronger and clearer in the ranks of the Fascist Party, is now confronting her destiny.[112]

And "Close observers of Fascism have, indeed, never doubted either its importance or its compatibility with the teaching of the Church."[113] Yet it would caution readers that "the hour is too early for any to judge how closely the corporate State will conform to the Holy Father's[114] farsighted axiom," and that "all activities, social and economic, virtually conscripted by the State, have yet to line up at work, as distinguished from the parade ground which they now fill in serried ranks of enthusiasts."[115] *Blackfriars* support of Fascism is instanced in strongly biased terms:

. . . if a Government calling itself Fascist introduces measures whereby Catholics are to be compelled to act against their consciences as propertly guided, . . . by the Church's dictum, then we as Catholics shall know that it can only be because, in that matter at any rate, it has been false to Fascism. . . . Fascism . . . is not a "policy" or a "program" . . . but a philosophy of citizenship, and preeminently a Christian philosophy, negativing the Pagan selfishness which, in the name of "individual liberty" or of "class consciousness" is ruining the world today.[116]

[112] James Barnes, "Fascism and the Catholic Church," *The Dublin Review*, CLXXV (July, 1924), 100–101.

[113] James Barnes, "Fascism and the International Centre of Fascist Studies," *The Dublin Review*, CLXXXV (October, 1929), 266.

[114] See *supra*, p. 64.

[115] M. Mansfield, "The Church and the Hour of Fascism," *The Dublin Review*, CLXXXI (July, 1927), 66.

[116] Quoted from a reprint of Herbert Shove, "Fascism and Religion," *The Catholic Mind*, XXXII (March 22, 1934), 119–120.

A note of chariness usually characterized *The Month's* comments on Fascism, and *The Christian Democrat* had the distinction of being fundamentally and consistently opposed to the Fascist movement. Contrary to most other organs of the Catholic press, *The Christian Democrat* gave space to, and supported, Don Luigi Sturso's Partito Populare.[117]

Social Services

Subscribing to the fundamental principle, reiterated by successive popes, "that individual men are of necessity the foundation, the cause and the reason for the existence of all social institutions";[118] acknowledging that "though Holy Church has the special task of sanctifying souls and making them partake of supernatural goods, she is also solicitous for the needs of men's daily life";[119] and understanding the twentieth-century challenge to the Church, viz., "the immense task of giving a human and Christian tone to modern civilization,"[120] the Social Catholic movement in England, from 1920 to 1955, interested itself in various aspects of the social services and in the amelioration of socioeconomic conditions. Its prime concern was, and remained, that the principle of subsidiarity be not violated—that the state control and administer only such services as could not be conducted adequately, efficiently, in keeping with the dignity of man as a human person made to the image of God, by lesser societies, organizations, and groups. Addressing the Liverpool branch of the Catholic Truth Society, March 11, 1921, Father Bede Jarrett, O.P., spoke on "State Interference and the Catholic Church," warning his audience against "the growing desire on the

---

[117] Cleary, *op. cit.,* p. 118.
[118] *Mater et Magistra,* p. 59.
[119] *Ibid.,* p. 4.
[120] *Ibid.,* p. 67.

part of the State to interfere with the liberty of the subject."[121]

Nevertheless, there was a growing realization of the need for a more comprehensive program of social service. At a conference on social service held in 1928, under the auspices of the Catholic Women's League, appeals were made for volunteer and professional workers in numerous areas of social service. And this, not as individuals or as members of private or religious groups, but in conjunction with the state organizations and under the direction of the local governments.[122]

A specific area in which the Social Catholic movement endeavored to exert its influence was that of housing. A Catholic housing association proposed in 1933 was envisioned as a means to "give a tremendous impetus to the spread and maintenance of the Faith in England."[123] It would counteract the breaking up of slum parishes by the state slum-clearance programs, for, the same author says:

> Should a slum-parish be threatened with dissolution through a sweeping clearance proposal, the Catholic Housing Association could step in, re-condition the property where possible, rebuild where necessary, and thus save the cost of a new church in an outlying suburb, while conserving the usefulness of the church already built.[124]

Though such an association never materialized, other interests in the housing problem achieved some organization. A movement in 1934 to ascertain the advantages and shortcomings of the existing housing facilities solicited the aid of the Catholic Social Guild study clubs and the Catholic Women's League in distributing questionnaires. This led to the

---

[121] "The State and Liberty," *The Tablet,* CXXXVIII (March 26, 1921) , 418.

[122] "A Conference on Social Studies," *The Tablet,* CLII (November 24, 1928) , 682.

[123] Thomas Foster, "A Catholic Housing Programme," *Blackfriars,* XIV (April, 1933) , 255.

[124] *Ibid.*

establishment of the Housing Enquiry Sub-committee under the auspices of the Catholic Social Guild. Its potential influence was evidenced by the attendance at a conference called by it in October of the founding year. Represented at the meeting were the following: Bethnal Green Housing Association, British Broadcasting Company, Catholic Transport Guilds, Church Army, Fabian Group, Guildhouse Women's Citizen's Society, Housing Centre, International Scientific Management Congress, National Council of Social Service, National Council of Women, National Women's Citizens' Association, St. Pancras House Improvement Society, Society of Women Housing Estate Managers, Southwark Housing Association, Westminster Housing Association, Westminister Housing Trust, Willesden Public Utility Society, Society of Friends, and the Catholic Social Guild. The subcommittee proved inadequate as the scope of interest and work widened, and it was decided that

> . . . a Council should be formed to watch housing schemes and new developments in planning and arrangement of houses, with a view to the comfort and convenience of working women, to stimulate interest among working women throughout the country and so to organize their opinion that public bodies may know what working women regard as essential to their homes, to do everything possible to maintain the standard of housing set out in the White Paper issued in 1919.[125]

Approximately two years later the decision was carried out in the formation of the Women's Advisory Housing Council. It was not a Catholic organization, though its officers included several Catholic Social Guild members, and the guild was affiliated to the council. It provided very directly a means whereby the Social Catholic movement could fulfill its aim of leavening society with Catholic principles.

---

[125] "Notes and Comments," *The Christian Democrat,* XIV (December, 1934) , 177.

As World War II wore on and the problem of postwar reconstruction loomed on the horizon, the Women's Advisory Housing Council focused its attention on the home of the future. Again the Catholic Social Study Clubs were called on for assistance in distributing questionnaires to determine the opinions of housewives on suitable and adequate housing. In this respect the English Catholic hierarchy had voiced its opinion in a joint pastoral letter of 1942, recommending that "the minimum living accommodation for a family should be such that no one has to sleep in the living room; that there be satisfactory sanitation; that there be a bathroom for each family. Slums should be abolished; there is no excuse for slums."[126]

In 1943 the Sword of the Spirit assumed the housing question as a special project. While is advocated cooperation with state building plans, it exhorted Catholics to "do all in their power to encourage choice and designing of the home, and to support all measures which secure the freedom of the individual and the welfare of the community."[127] It proposed by the education of youth and adults "to develop the orderly and seemly usage of the modern scientific facilities for the home."[128] In place of the materialistic outlook, a Christian attitude should be cultivated, so that

> comfort should be sought so that life may be lifted from the rut of drudgery onto a higher spiritual plane. Space and privacy should guard the decencies of life. . . . Beauty and order should become connected with the idea of peace and combine to create a truly Catholic atmosphere.[129]

[126] "Joint Pastoral Letter of the Hierarchy of England and Wales," July, 1942. Quoted in Gordon, *Security, Freedom and Happiness,* p. 205.

[127] "The Catholic and the Housing Question," Sword Paper No. 13, *Sword of the Spirit Bulletin,* No. 58 (June 3, 1943), 5.

[128] *Ibid.*

[129] *Ibid.*

With these basic ideas in mind, the Sword of the Spirit Sub-committee drew up a rather comprehensive and detailed plan of what building and renovating of homes in the postwar era should include. It was guided in all its recommendations by the joint pastoral letter of the English hierarchy of July, 1942. Warning against secularism, J. N. Gibson declared that "the Catholic who divorces the housing problem from the nature of man, made in God's image, apes the material-ist. . . ."[130] In the era when England had launched its welfare state system, and in view of the difficulties encountered in its housing scheme, Gibson envisaged the following program as practicable for Catholics:

> . . . study the technicalities of the housing problem; help to solve it by (1) pressing for a higher priority; (2) moderating the undue raising of minimum standards . . . ; (3) opposing the increasingly heavy taxation of houses; (4) advocating a solution of rent control that does justice to both sides.[131]

With the economic adversity of the 1930's came, of necessity, extended state programs of social service. By 1934 it spent approximately £500,000,000 a year on benefits including free education, old-age pensions, medical service, and unemployment allowances. At the time it was valued as a "good and necessary work."[132] The continued expansion of these services drew criticism from various sources, but particularly from Catholics. Lord Amulree, addressing the Royal Society of Arts, drew attention to the implication of extended government control and believed "the question of the immediate future will be how far genuine freedom of choice will be

---

[130] "The Housing Problem," *Catholic Social Guild Leaflet*, No. 35 (1949), n.p.

[131] *Ibid.*

[132] "News and Notes," *The Tablet*, CLXIV (December 15, 1934), 771.

maintained in a country in which that choice has increasing consequences for the public purse. . . ."[133] According to Lord Amulree, everything that had passed in the last twenty-five years "confirmed the arguments"[134] of Hilaire Belloc in *The Servile State.* Lord Amulree saw a totalitarianism developing under the guise of a "completely virtuous humanitarian democracy."[135] The social-service program, he asserted, created a proletarian climate unpropitious "for the growth of religious truth, which is essentially concerned with the recognition of responsibility. . . ."[136]

The publication of the Beveridge Report[137] in 1942 evoked

---

[133] "Liberty and Social Services," *The Tablet,* CLXX (November 6, 1937), 616.

[134] *Ibid.*

[135] *Ibid.,* 617.

[136] *Ibid.*

[137] Inconsistencies in the existing program manifested the need for integration; inadequacy in some areas evidenced the need for reorganization and expansion. Accordingly, Sir William Beveridge in 1941 was appointed head of a commission to investigate the situation ("Britain's Cradle to Grave Security," *America,* LXXIX [July 17, 1948], 388). "One fundamental concept underlies the whole Report. That is the national minimum—a basic income which . . . every citizen of Great Britain will receive in the event of old age, sickness, unemployment, or other vicissitudes, an income toward which he will have contributed and which is his by right of contract. Along with this goes the proposal for the administration of insurance and assistance by one organization, a Ministry of Social Security, with a single contribution by the insured person and a series of benefits built upon one calculated base.

"This aim is to be achieved through the use of the existing pattern of social insurance, supplemented by private insurance and assistance, and accompanied by a system of allowances for every child after the first child . . . and including the first child where there is an interruption of earnings. . . . The Report makes a fundamental recommendation, . . . that a comprehensive national health service be developed which will 'ensure that for every citizen there is available whatever medical treatment he requires, . . . domiciliary or institutional, general, specialist or consultant, and will ensure also

further controversy. In general, rationalization pro and con pursued rather specific lines. Michael P. Fogarty and Father Andrew Gordon, S.J., give the gist of favorable arguments: "The more I study the Beveridge Report, the more I am convinced that it provided a solution to the problems of social insurance. . . ."[138] and "We have read and studied the Beveridge Report and our conclusion is that it is based on sound principles and has much to commend it. . . ."[139] The trends of the adverse arguments, which were more extensively carried on, are given by the same authors. The one is the principle of subsidiarity—"What can well be left to private initiative should be left";[140] the other is the basic idea of the living wage—"If the government is ignoring the Living Wage and offering us the Beveridge Report in its stead, then we are definitely further on our way to the 'Servile State' prophesied long ago by Mr. Hilaire Belloc."[141]

The Tablet deplored "the proposal for a Ministry of Social Security, with the elimination . . . of the many agencies which have hitherto been active in this field."[142] It, too, saw in the Beveridge Plan the fulfillment of the Belloc's predictions in *The Servile State*. It admonished the populace to keep in mind two principles:

(1) That all these reports in their different fields will produce accumulatively a result much more oppressive

---

the provision of dental, ophthalmic and surgical appliances, nursing and midwifery and rehabilitation after accidents'" (Karl de Schweinitz, *England's Road to Social Security* [Philadelphia: University of Pennsylvania Press, 1943], pp. 230–231).

[138] Michael P. Fogarty, "The Beveridge Report," *The Christian Democrat*, XXIII (January, 1943), 2.

[139] Gordon, *op cit.*, p. 90.

[140] Fogarty, "The Beveridge Report," 2.

[141] Gordon, *op. cit.*, p. 90.

[142] "The Beveridge Report," *The Tablet*, CLXXX (December 5, 1942), 271.

and totalitarian than any of the authors, each applying the same principle, of more State control in his own field, has intended or envisaged; and

(2) That the best security against the abuse of power lies in the existence of all manner of different organizations for different social purposes, all under the common law.[143]

As the government issued white papers for clarification, and as laws to implement the recommendations were progressively enacted, *The Tablet* did not change its opinion. It continued to brand the Beveridge Plan as a compulsory, lifelong contract, subjecting the individual to complete subservience, for "a workman will be in a very weak position if a single authority keeps all the details of his employment history and his medical history on one card, and holds his savings as hostage for his docility in accepting official suggestions."[144] It further contended that the Plan

> does not reach the really poor, because they cannot be expected to pay the contributions, and therefore must not be given the benefits, because that would be unfair to those who pay. At the lowest level, the Plan does not apply; and yet it is always in the name of the really poorest section that the Plan is recommended. . . . It can hardly be too often repeated that the chief item for which this money is collected . . . is not insurance against unemployment, but insurance toward retirement pensions.[145]

According to *The Tablet,* "there never was a time when Christians more needed to have the understanding, as well as the courage, of their own convictions and traditions."[146] It called upon Christians to reinstate their ideals to thwart the

---

[143] *Ibid.,* 272.

[144] "The Salesmen of Servitude," *The Tablet,* CLXXXI (June 19, 1943), 291.

[145] *Ibid.*

[146] "Christian Pluralism," *The Tablet,* CLXXXIII (June 17, 1944), 291.

imminent totalitarian control "which is able to direct all the national energies at will"[147] and, by a series of legally enforced obligations, is able to direct the life of the individual so as to make of it "a tramway journey, planned and predestined from start to finish."[148]

Welfare State. As the realization of the Beveridge proposals approached in the passage of the National Insurance Act and the National Health Service Act, both in 1946, the hierarchy of England and Wales issued the following statement:

> We are agreed that the best possible hospital service should be available to every citizen. We are also agreed that voluntary effort in this country should be encouraged and not curtailed. To achieve this double purpose and to protect certain basic moral principles we consider that the following amendments should be made in the National Health Service Bill:
>
> 1. To protect the rights of ownership, the premises, endowments, trusts of a voluntary hospital should continue to be vested in the trustees or management committee of the hospital.
> 2. To protect the purpose or trust for which the voluntary hospital was originally founded:
>   (a) A voluntary hospital should retain its own management committee, with absolute freedom to appoint its medical and nursing staff from persons properly qualified, and
>   (b) absolute freedom to apply its funds, whether received from the Government or endowment or subscription, for the general purposes of the hospital.
>   (c) In the event of the Minister's being unable or unwilling to accept these proposals, voluntary hospitals should have the right to contract out of the scheme.

---

[147] *Ibid.*
[148] *Ibid.*

3. To safeguard the conscience of a medical practitioner a clause should be inserted in the Bill by which no medical practitioner should be penalized for being unable or unwilling to act against his conscience.[149]

To some extent the statement set the tone for the attitude of the Social Catholic movement toward what came to be known as the welfare state. The Social Catholic movement never ceased to point out, and warn against, various aspects which is deemed contrary to Catholic principles. In an article entitled "First Things First," Father Paul Crane, S.J., censured not

central planning as such, but a certain type of argument employed in its defence, namely that which judges it primarily in terms of its ability to confer benefits and only secondarily, if at all, in terms of its effect on man as a human person, possessed of intelligence and will and meant to act freely and with responsibility. Such an attitude . . . is dangerous. It opens the gate wide to a subtle kind of totalitarianism. . . .[150]

The Catholic Social Guild was foremost in voicing its deprecations; leaflets and articles in *The Christian Democrat* left no doubt as to its stand on the welfare state. Criticisms were leveled at the materialistic outlook of the system, the lack of initiative and the loss of a sense of responsibility which the plan engendered, the creation of a proletariat, the totalitarianism inherent in the extended state control, the violation of the principle of subsidiarity, the nationalization of industries, the exploitation of the system for vote-getting, and the lowering of standards among social workers.[151] In contrast, Michael

[149] Quoted in "The National Health Service Bill," *The Tablet,* CLXXXVII (May 11, 1946), 242.

[150] *Catholic Social Guild Leaflet,* No. 30 (1948), n.p.

[151] There is considerable overlapping in the pertinent articles, but some of the more specific titles may be cited: Samuel Sanderson, "Reflections on National Insurance," *Catholic Social Guild Leaflet,* No.

P. Fogarty boldly wrote, "I like the Welfare State."[152] The author saw minor flaws, but in general he considered the welfare state the means of the state in fulfilling its obligation to "direct, watch, stimulate, and restrain, as circumstances may require. . . ."[153] Within six years Fogarty saw the situation differently, and another article appeared, this time entitled "Reforming the Welfare State."[154] Lord Iddesleigh could "find no Catholic authority against, and much in favour of, the Welfare State."[155] In his opinion, "the relief of the sick and poor by Government action . . . was in line with the tradition of the royal saints—Edward, Henry, Stephen and Lewis—who founded hospitals and schools with public money, curbed the wealthy and the powerful and defended the poor."[156] The idea of the state practicing the corporal works of mercy succinctly epitomizes the Social Catholic movement's limited approval of the welfare state.

Catholic opinions and attitudes are learned predominantly through the press. But it is the Catholic press, too, which largely forms and directs Catholic opinions and attitudes. The organs of the Catholic press are, in turn, frequently the official organs of societies and organizations. A study of the activities of various associations on behalf of the Social Catholic movement forms the core of the succeeding chapter.

---

21 (1948); Dorothy Sarmiento, "A Social Worker Looks at the National Health Service," *Catholic Social Guild Leaflet,* No. 27 (1948); C. Lucey, "The Ethics of Nationalization," *Catholic Social Guild Leaflet,* No. 13 (1947); John D'Alton, "The Catholic Church and Freedom," II, *The Christian Democrat,* new ser., III (May, 1952), 106–108; Paul Crane, "Auctioneering," *The Christian Democrat,* new ser., X (September–October, 1959), 449–450.

152 *The Christian Democrat,* new ser., II (November, 1951), 256–259.

153 *Ibid.,* 256.

154 *The Tablet,* CCIX (May 25, 1957), 485–486.

155 "A Catholic in Politics," *Blackfriars,* XXXII (March, 1951), 105.

156 *Ibid.,* 105–106.

Chapter III

FORMATION AND ACTIVITY OF
VARIOUS ORGANIZATIONS

Haphazard, individual efforts would have availed little in
the Social Catholic movement. Concerted thought and study,
and planned activity, were necessary. These were provided by
various organizations. Some, founded explicitly to function as
part of the Social Catholic movement, had their origin prior
to the period 1920–1955, the period covered in this study.
Their inception and initial undertakings were considered in
Chapter I; hence, this section will be concerned with their further development and continued activity. Organizations of
more recent origin will be studied from their incipience, and
others, assuming responsibility in the social apostolate in the
period under consideration, will be reviewed to the extent
of their participation in the Social Catholic movement.

Catholic Social Guild

As in the World War I decade, so in the years 1920–1955
the Catholic Social Guild was in the vanguard of the Social
Catholic movement. Seasonally its pristine fervor and enthusiasm waned, but its resurgence was always prompt. Through
the vicissitudes of the between-the-war years the Catholic
Social Guild steadfastly pursued the aims[1] set forth at its
foundation. By 1920 it was evident that further implementation of the "means"[2] was requisite to achieve its aims on a

---

[1] *Supra,* p. 17.
[2] *Ibid.*

broader scale. Correspondingly, it embarked upon new ventures.

Summer Schools. A novel enterprise of the Catholic Social Guild was the summer school, which made its debut in 1920. Thereafter it was held annually for one week, except for the war years, when it was limited to a week-end. It was envisioned as a means of bringing together all classes, of promoting understanding between employers and employees, of bringing Catholic social teaching to an ever-widening circle. The fifty men and women who attended the initial summer school were a diverse group:

> There were miners and shipyard men, postal workers, textile workers, railwaymen, engineers, clerks and shopkeepers. There was a Labour Exchange manager and the manager of an industrial concern. Nearly all were young men and wage-earners actively connected with trade-unions, co-operative societies and Catholic organizations. Many were members of local authorities, and in most cases leading members of study-clubs.[3]

It set a precedent and any one year could claim as great a diversity in its enrollment. The second summer school registered "a major-general and three colonels, a professor of theology and three Jesuits, a miner and three railwaymen, cotton-workers from Rochdale, engineers from Clydeside and teachers."[4] Attendance increased year by year, until the school of 1948 claimed a record 230 members. A gradual decline set in after this, and the divergence in the Catholic Social Guild in the late fifties had repercussions that led to a dearth of applicants for the summer schools, and cancellations resulted.

The summer school had a set schedule, with minor variations from year to year. Each week was opened with a sermon

---

[3] *Catholic Social Year Book, 1922,* p. 29.
[4] Cleary, *op. cit.,* p. 89.

by a renowned preacher. Series of lectures carried through the week. Each day there were periods of informal discussion which were considered invaluable for exchange of ideas, for the introduction of new projects, and for mutual encouragement in the social apostolate. It was during the informal discussion of the maiden meeting that guild members came to the decision and made definite plans for the launching of *The Christian Democrat* and the Catholic Workers' College.[5]

The lectures were centered on definite topics—usually current problems—and the pertinent Catholic social teaching was expounded, and practical applications indicated. Eminent lecturers gave generously of their time and knowledge to help make the summer schools a worthwhile, inspiring, learning, and practical experience. Among the noted speakers through the years were such renowned individuals as Father Martindale, S.J., Father Vincent McNabb, O.P., Maisie Ward, John Eppstein, Father Lewis Watt, S.J., Michael P. Fogarty, Barbara Ward; and from foreign shores, Father John A. Ryan of the United States, Père Guitton, S.J., of France, Dr. P. J. Serrarens of Holland, and Father Perquy, O. P., of Belgium. A listing of some of one speaker's themes will illustrate the gamut of topics considered by the summer school gatherings. Father Lewis Watt, enthusiastic and effective in lecturing, treated of strikes (1926); the state and the citizen (1927); ethics (1928); *Rerum Novarum* (1929); the future of capitalism (1931); Marxian socialism (1932); the moral law with reference to *Quadragesimo Anno* (1933); the state (1934); Henry George (1935); an introduction to the study of *Quadragesimo Anno* (1936); usury (1937); the development of the papal social teaching from 1891 to the present day (1941); and family allowances (1942).

Enthusiasm ran high at the summer schools, and members carried away with them fresh inspiration, new ideas, new

---

[5] *Ibid.*, p. 61.

learning, renewed fervor, rejuvenated interest to carry on the social apostolate through study clubs, in their places of employment, in the local governments, and wherever it was possible to make their spirit a recognized influence. Nevertheless, the school had its critics. Writing in 1926, Father Vincent McNabb, in his conviction that social reform was possible only by a return to the land, saw the summer schools only as offering a plan of superficial amelioration rather than a plan that would eradicate the sources of the social evils:

> Many of the expedients suggested . . . are but attempts to cure the defects of bad circumstances, not by a change of circumstances, but a change of medicine. If only you can draw your audience's attention to a necessity for nations, like individuals, to fly the occasion of sin, you will soon pass from discussing that Race Suicide which is the shortest way out; and you will begin to discuss economic evil in terms of the city, where these evils are forced to breed. . . . In other words, you will discuss the exodus which alone can justify us before the God who gave the land into our keeping.[6]

Another critic saw the summer school as

> . . . a publicity venture; a means of advertisement. Attention, indeed, was focused on one topic, with the design of inspiring study and ameliorative effort in the direction of industrial relations; but the real advertisement was . . . for the Catholic Social Guild. It was meant to maintain the confidence of the members in the value of the work they were doing, and to gain new supporters for the cause.
>
> During the whole week the Catholic Social Guild was, as it were, open to public view. Its purposes, its methods, its effect stood clear. It is essentially a teaching body.[7]

The good accomplished by the summer schools, though un-

---

[6] Vincent McNabb, *The Church and the Land* (London: Burns, Oates & Washbourne, Ltd., 1926) , pp. 166–167.

[7] Maurice Gaffney, "Social Guild Summer School," *The Irish Monthly*, LXXIX (November, 1951) , 474.

measurable, definitely contributed to the Social Catholic movement. Their discontinuance in the late fifties can be attributed to the internal difficulties of the Catholic Social Guild rather than to their futility.

An Official Organ. Following the decision made at the first summer school in 1920, there appeared in January, 1921, the first issue of the new monthly publication, *The Christian Democrat,* which fulfilled

> a triple aim, forming a link between study-clubs and members, giving the study-clubs matter for thought outside their current textbooks, and providing popular social instruction for those who feel that they have no opportunity for regular study.[8]

The initial number carried the editor's statement that as Christian Democrats they had adopted a program[9] and that the new organ would expound the points "with greater fulness and with application to present-day questions. . . ."[10] Vagueness and unreality were to be shunned, for, said the editor, "dealing as we shall be with practical and concrete questions, we shall often be concerned with details, with schemes and systems, with matters of machinery and organisation."[11] Besides the topics comprised in the program, *The Christian Democrat* dealt with diverse current problems and social conditions, as indicated in Chapter II. Its foresight and insight into social problems was exemplified in its exposition of plans, such as family allowances, far in advance of others. Its adamantine stand on subjects that had become controversial in England, e.g., Fascism and Distributism, revealed a comprehension of basic political, social, and economic principles. Under the editorship of Henry Somerville, 1921–1923, and Father

[8] Cleary, *op. cit.,* p. 112.

[9] *Supra,* p. 30.

[10] Henry Somerville, "What We Are," *The Christian Democrat,* I (January, 1921), 3.

[11] *Ibid.*

84

Leo O'Hea, S.J., 1924–1946, *The Christian Democrat,* as the official organ, reflected the views and the position of the Catholic Social Guild. After World War II, when Father Paul Crane, S.J., became editor in 1947, and particularly with the new format of *The Christian Democrat* in 1950 , a breach was manifested. The inside front cover prominently bore the statement: "The views expressed in *The Christian Democrat* are those of the writers themselves and not necessarily to be attributed to the Catholic Social Guild under whose auspices it is published." Articles, and other publications also, frequently were marked: "This is written by request to promote discussion. The Guild is not committed to any views here expressed."[12] For several years the brief and few references to the guild were confined to the covers of *The Christian Democrat.* The growing dichotomy presaged the reorganization of the Catholic Social Guild necessitated a few years after 1955. In that revamping, harmony of opinion and concerted effort— a return to the founding spirit—were emphasized, and in January, 1960, the new editor, Robert P. Walsh, stated: "First of all *The Christian Democrat* is the organ of the Catholic Social Guild, and the Guild is the official body of the Catholic Church in the field of social action. . . . The Guild is a teaching body and *The Christian Democrat* is one of its means of teaching."[13]

But prior to the rift within the organization the need for appraisal of the guild's capacity to meet the demands of the times was obvious. The aftermath of World War II, accompanied by the revolutionary changes in the governmental social welfare policy, and the full-employment atmosphere, coupled with a realization of the duty to serve all Catholics,[14] compelled some change if the Guild was to remain an effective

[12] These comments can be found in various issues of the 1950's.

[13] *The Christian Democrat,* new ser. XI, 1–2 (1960) .

[14] William F. Ryan, "C. S. G. and the Welfare State," *Social Order,* V (June, 1955) , 267.

instrument in the Social Catholic movement. It could no longer aim merely "to facilitate intercourse between Catholic students and workers" and "to assist in working out the application of Catholic principles to actual social conditions."[15] It took on broader, more comprehensive implications, so that it aimed "to train its members for the Catholic Social Apostolate" and "to develop among members a sound knowledge of Catholic social principles and teaching and their application to current social problems in public and private life."[16] The "means" were retained, but the provision "by encouraging Catholics to take their due share in public life, and generally by co-operation with other societies"[17] were added.

Catholic Workers' College. As a "teaching body," one of the most significant undertakings of the Catholic Social Guild was the establishment of the Catholic Workers' College in 1921. It had been envisioned by Father Plater, but it materialized only after his death, as a memorial to the Guild founder's distinguished work in the social apostolate. The objectives of the College were to provide residential university teaching in the social sciences for adult wage earners of elementary education and to train them for leadership within their own class. Father Leo O'Hea, S.J., the first principal, commented: "We expect them to return to their respective trades with the spirit of the apostolate, ready and qualified to bring the Church's principles of social welfare to their fellow men."[18] Approval of the hierarchy of England and Wales had been secured, and when, in October, 1921, Father O'Hea and three students—a locomotive driver, a sheet metal worker, and a textile worker—arrived in Oxford and took up lodgings at 223 Ifley Road, the college was instituted. No official title had been designated—it was simply the Catholic Workers' College.

---

[15] Statutes of the Catholic Social Guild, 1926.
[16] Statutes of the Catholic Social Guild, 1949.
[17] *Ibid.*
[18] Quoted in "Notes," *The Tablet,* CXXXIX (January 7, 1922), 9.

The College was welcomed at Oxford and, from its beginning, had influential and true friends who were ready to advise, guide, assist with teaching, and, at times, assist with
finances: A. D. Lindsay and G. N. Clark, head of Balliol and
head of Oriel, respectively; Dr. A. J. Carlyle, Fellow and
Tutor of University College; G. D. H. Cole; Henry Sander-
son-Furniss, Principal of Ruskin College; F. F. Urquhart,
Fellow of Balliol; and Blackfriars and Campion Hall, whose
members gave freely of their time and tutorial services. It
was Dr. A. J. Carlyle "who took the College under his wing
and offered suggestions which formed the general plan of
studies in the Catholic Workers' College for over thirty
years."[19] The courses offered included social ethics; moral
philosophy; philosophy of religion; economic theory, organization, and history; political theory and organization; and such
special subjects as trade unions, local government, and international relations. In 1925 the college was recognized by the
Board of Education, under its Adult Education Regulations,
"as a Society or Institution in Oxford established for the purposes of higher study,"[20] and students thenceforth were entitled to the diploma studies.[21] This involved an examination
consisting of "six three-hour papers, Economic Theory, Modern Economic Organization, The Economic History of England from 1660, Political Science and Political Organization,
and a sixth Subject at choice, usually, . . . The History,
Theory and Practice of Trade Unions."[22]

At the beginning of the second year the college took up
residence at Walton Well Road. Soon after, the guild offices
moved to the same location, and until 1950 both were admin-

[19] Cleary, *op. cit.,* p. 127.
[20] "The Catholic Workers' College, Principal's Report" (July
25, 1926), 5.
[21] Previously, "college men under twenty-five, and all women, had
been debarred from the examinations, and those who entered did
so as private students" (Cleary, *op. cit.,* p. 129) .
[22] "College News," *The Christian Democrat,* VI (July, 1926) , 115.

istered by the same staff, though financial accounts were kept separate. More space was made available to students when the Catholic Social Guild moved to Woodstock Road, and in 1955 the newly acquired and renovated building at Boars Hill, named Plater Hall, provided accommodations for twenty-four students. During World War II the college was suspended, and the residence at Walton Well Road "was given up to nursing-mothers evacuated from London."[23] The "parting of ways" of the Catholic Social Guild and the Catholic Workers' College was another indication of the "departmental individualism" which was catalytic in disrupting the centripetal program devised by the founders of the Catholic Social Guild.[24] Students who came to the college after the war illustrated the forthcoming cleavage. Unlike prewar students, the majority knew nothing, or little, of the Catholic Social Guild, nor had they been members of study clubs prior to coming to Oxford. Furthermore, some students demanded "to use their college years to qualify for a career in one of the newer social services. . . ."[25] This entailed some reorganization of the curriculum and taking the university diploma in public and social administration rather than in economics and political science.

In 1923 the College opened its doors to the first women students. Living accommodations for them were provided by Margaret Fletcher, who took them into her home. It was the women on the Executive Committee of the Catholic Social Guild who furthered the cause of the working women stu-

---

[23] Cleary, *op. cit.,* p. 176.

[24] Shortly before his death Father Plater drew up the following program for the Guild: "(1) A Catholic Social Magazine. (2) A Catholic Workers' College at Oxford. (3) A Flood of Catholic Social Literature. (4) Organisers for the North of England. (5) Multiplication of Study Circles" ("Notes and Comments," *The Christian Democrat,* I [March, 1921], 9).

[25] Cleary, *op. cit.,* p. 217.

88

dents, realizing that "working women need leaders from their own class."[26] Miss Fletcher saw in the working women a potential influence for good; education was necessary to activate it:

Working women showed themselves very courageous in upholding their faith when publicly attacked, and some were very effective speakers; but it was becoming more and more clear that a few of them when educated as this College could educate them, would have an immense influence for good in the factory and the shop or wherever their work took them. There would be no spectacular results. It would be a slow permeation by truth.[27]

Response from Catholic Women's Societies to appeals for scholarship funds was generous, the Catholic Women's League being foremost in consistently answering appeals.

All students attended the College on a scholarship basis. The funds were secured from various sources: the Catholic Young Men's Society, the Knights of St. Columba, Catholic Social Guild branches, study clubs, the working men themselves, and individuals of means—all contributed to the financing of the education of the Catholic Workers' College students. In addition, from 1926 on, the students were eligible for a Board of Education grant, at a maximum of £20 per annum, determined "by *inter alia* (i) the cost, standard, and efficiency of the work as shown by inspection and by the Prospectus, Report and other returns, and (ii) the extent to which the teaching staff and the more advanced students are successful in adding to knowledge."[28] After the war there were other sources of financial assistance available. Local education authorities made generous grants "to individual stu-

---

[26] Margaret Fletcher, M. L. Blackledge, Annie Holmes, "The Women's Side of the Catholic Workers' College," *The Christian Democrat,* II (April, 1922), 14.

[27] Quoted in Cleary, *op cit.,* p. 128, from Miss Fletcher's autobiography, *O, Call Back Yesterday* (Oxford: Blackwell, 1939).

[28] "College News," *The Christian Democrat,* VI (July, 1926), 116.

dents towards their costs of rail fares, clothes, books and personal expenses. . . ."[29] In 1956 grants to students from various public authorities totaled £4,000.[30] An allocation totaling £1,700 from the Ministry of Education was also reported for the year 1948-1949.[31] In the 1950's these grants approximated £2,500 per annum.[32]

Screening of applicants was imperative, and from the beginning the student body was carefully selected. The purpose of the College—"to train adult wage-earners for social leadership in the ordinary surroundings of working-class life, for action, instruction, guidance among Catholic and non-Catholic people, for work which students of other classes cannot do at all or cannot do so well"[33]—had always to be kept in mind when selecting students from among the many applicants. A number of factors required consideration:

> The candidate's occupation should be more or less typical of his home neighbourhood, and he should have reasonable prospects of being able to regain employment after a year or two at Oxford. He should have some personality and disposition for leadership in the small opportunities that may have come his way. He must have some aptitude and desire for study, readiness to make use of what limited facilities may have been available for him, for example, in the study clubs of the Guild.[34]

Selection of students continued to be made on the same basis, but the changed conditions following the war required some alteration to keep the College abreast of the times.

---

29 "The Catholic Workers' College, Report for the Year 1948-49," 3.

30 Cleary, *op. cit.,* p. 216.

31 "The Catholic Workers' College, Report for the Year 1948-49," 3.

32 Cleary, *op. cit.,* p. 216.

33 "Notes and Comments," *The Christian Democrat,* XIX (March, 1939), 38.

34 *Ibid.*

Accordingly, adult students of other types and from other backgrounds were to be admitted. It was acknowledged that "much good may be promoted by training Catholics who are preparing for, or who hold, administrative positions in industry."[35] More extensive use of the course offered was to be encouraged, as were contacts between college and university members. Besides, it was considered advisable that "shorter courses should also be provided for study club leaders and others and, in particular, 'refresher' courses for past students."[36] It is interesting to note the occupations represented by students; in the year 1948–1949 the list read: "clerical, engineering, electrical, iron foundry, shop assistant, waiter, joiners, vehicle builder, teacher, cabinet maker, boys' home worker, traveller, draughtsman, miner, transport."[37] In 1949–1950 the list included bricklayer, laboratory worker, journalist, printer, toolmaker, milkman, spinner, welder, and chemical worker.[38] While most students came from England, Scotland, and Wales, foreign countries were also represented in the later years. For instance, in 1952 there were two students from Germany, one from British Guiana, and one—a priest—from India; and in 1957, Tanganyika, India, Vietnam, Ireland, and Malta sent students.

Commenting on the objectives of the projected Workers' College in April, 1921, *The Tablet* anticipated that the students would become

. . . efficient and leading workers in all departments of Catholic activity proper to laymen, such as the St. Vincent de Paul Society, the Catholic Young Men's Society, the

[35] "Report of the Thirty-fifth Annual Meeting, Catholic Social Guild" (July 30, 1944), 5.

[36] *Ibid.*

[37] "The Catholic Workers' College, Report for the Year 1948–49," 3.

[38] "The Catholic Workers' College, Report for the Year 1949–50," 3.

Catholic Federation, the Catholic Social Guild, and so forth. They will also be fitted to advance Catholic interests in public life and in Labour organizations.[39]

During the college's first twenty-five years of operation, 146 students had been guided, counseled, taught—prepared to take their place of influence when they returned to the work-a-day world. There are no statistics to measure the spiritual influence nor to show the extent to which Catholic social principles were disseminated by the college alumni. However, the occupational areas to which they returned, the leadership which they assumed, and the public offices which many acquired, afforded ample opportunity to promulgate Catholic social teaching. A survey of the seventy-three men and thirteen women who attended the college up to 1939 yielded the following information:

> . . . 20 stayed only for one year. Over 75 per cent passed the diploma examination. Of 71 men whose careers can be traced, 26 changed their occupations. 1 became Organising Secretary of C.S.G., 2 became priests (7 men and 1 woman took university degrees) ; 1 became a university lecturer, 1 a tutor at the College, 5 became teachers. There was 1 M.P. and 2 Trade Union officials. 3 men became Officers of the National Assistance Board, 2 went to the Ministry of Labour, 1 to the Ministry of National Insurance. One, a miner disabled by a pit accident, became a Registrar of births, marriages, and deaths. 1 became a Factory Inspector, 2 went to training within industry, 1 is a Probation Officer and 1 joined the Inland Revenue. Of the 71 mentioned, 40 were active in 1952, and 14 had a record of past activity. Almost the same number were active in C.S.G., 15 of them being branch officials and 7 serving on the Executive Committee. 17 were in office in Trade unions, and many were doing good work at ordi-

---

[39] "Proposed Catholic Labour College," *The Tablet,* CXXXVIII (April 23, 1921), 542.

nary member level. Approximately 30 were active in politics.[40]

This résumé does not disclose the tremendous work done in study clubs, in other societies, Catholic and non-Catholic, as lecturers, and as contributors to magazines. A study of the postwar students would reveal a similar pattern of activity—College-trained men holding political positions and social welfare offices, leading in trade unions, active in societies, conducting study clubs, lecturing and writing. But the number was always too small, and the Catholic Workers' College and its accomplishments remained relatively unknown in England.[41]

Study Clubs. As the fortunes of the Catholic Social Guild fluctuated, so did its activities and undertakings. While the study club, circle, or action group remained an outstanding educative means of inculcating Catholic social principles, it also flourished and waned. In general, the study clubs were short-lived, although of the 129 clubs active in 1931, 50 "were in their third successive year and some had an unbroken history for eight or nine years."[42] Where the clergy undertook the leadership of the clubs, the duration and success tended to be greater. Trained lay tutors and ex-college students also conducted clubs successfully, but unfortunately, many clubs were forced to rely exclusively on outlines, textbooks, and other suggestions for guidance in their study. The difficulties

---

[40] Cleary, *op cit.,* p. 152, n. Quoted by the author "from a long memorandum printed in the Catholic Workers' College minutes under the date March 29th, 1952."

[41] Whitaker's Almanac now includes the Catholic Workers' College in its list of long-term residential colleges, under Adult Education, but a "Handbook that was meant to be 'a complete and up-to-date directory of Catholic schools and educational institutions'" (1961) made no mention of it. (Cleary, *op. cit.,* p. 217, n).

[42] Cleary, *op. cit.,* p. 99.

and problems involved in such a procedure are obvious, and it is remarkable that the clubs accomplished as much as they did. Despite the interest in study clubs, their membership remained out of proportion to the total membership, which was largely benevolent and inactive; for instance, in 1930 there were 2,135 Guild members; of these, only 610 were members of a study club (there were 104 study clubs). There was an eagerness to learn among study group members, but hesitancy in taking the adult examinations for certification persisted. Correspondence tuition and school study of social problems increased through the years, but it was the young student who sat for the examinations, not the adult. The following table gives an interesting profile of the situation during the period under study in this paper.

An active, enthusiastic study club found numerous opportunities of disseminating the Church's social teaching. Study was not an end in itself; it led to action. Indicative of this was St. Joseph's Study Club in Salford, 1933–1935, conducted by John Ford, an ex-college student. Its membership included plumbers, sheet metal workers, slaters, dockers, clerks, a rubbishman, a postman, and some unemployed men. The accompanying chart depicts the social impact made possible by the club's contacts. The ample opportunities for translating learning into activity to meet and influence others is further exemplified in the "Study Club News," for years a monthly feature of *The Christian Democrat*. Random reports will illustrate:

> Clitheroe SS. Michael and John, twelve members, work on *Quadragesimo Anno* under Mr. B. Winckley; the circle has conducted a door-to-door canvass for Catholic newspapers, issues a quarterly magazine *The Booklet*, arranges fortnightly debates and lectures in winter, duplicates its own handbills, has formed a lending library for the parish, makes sure reports of all activities appear

TABLE 1
PROFILE OF EDUCATIONAL ACTIVITIES OF THE C.S.G.

YEAR	MEMBER-SHIP	NO. OF STUDY CLUBS	CORRES-PONDENCE	ADULT EXAMIN-ATIONS	SCHOOL EXAMIN-ATIONS
1921	1,950	81	58	58	....
1922	1,881	160	59	75	....
1923	2,184	120	34	30	....
1924	2,359	165	38	14	....
1925	2,500	163	42	44	....
1926	2,523	117	29	37	....
1927	2,684	127	21	53	....
1928	2,589	109	7	41	....
1929	2,352	100	4	8	....
1930	2,135	104	6	13	....
1931	2,403	129	4	24	142
1932	2,495	149	2	36	60
1933	2,613	212	22	56	113
1934	2,795	228	10	24	122
1935	2,812	200	8	16	148
1936	3,095	230	12	17	160
1937	3,377	330	17	11	166
1938	3,661	379	14	39	162
1939	3,910	329	35	28	183
1940	3,443	180	5	....	106
1941	2,962	113	5	11	54
1942	3,228	147	7	15	180
1943	3,510	244	1	2	222
1944	3,560	....	2	13	222
1945	3,795	....	34	7	213
1946	3,502	82	42	9	179
1947	4,055	220	100	15	158
1948	4,166	284	118	55	102
1949	3,866	300+	200	150+	135
1950	3,528	337	155	155	229
1951	3,836	200+	167	238	235
1952	3,403	172	220	219	285
1953	3,663	125	....	332	384
1954	3,986	119*	....	206	457
1955	4,120	96	....	232	688

*Study clubs became known as action groups.

FIGURE 1

The Contacts of an Active Study-club[43]

Political

Talks to Conservative Party

Talks to Labour Party

Catholic Members of Labour
Party

Special Group

Knights of Saint Columba

Officers' Group

Squires' Group

Local Government

Alderman T. Evason

Councillor C. Goodall

St. Joseph's
Study Group

The Link Society,
which helped with
One-day schools
Week-end schools
Social Week.

Trade Unions

Municipal & General Workers Union

Transport & General Workers Union

Sheet Metal Workers

Plumbers

Press

Weekly report in *Salford City Reporter*

Responsible for Salford distribution of
Catholic Worker

Society of Saint Vincent
de Paul

---

[43] Reproduced from Cleary, *op. cit.,* p. 157.

96

in the local press, and sees that no anti-Catholic press letter goes unanswered.

London and South . . . St. Leonard's-on-Sea C.S.L. circle, eight members taking *Code of International Ethics* under Fr. D. Greenstock, runs a girls' club, a work party for the Distressed Areas and starts a "Home-Making" campaign to bring back interest and pride in the "home-made" article; demonstrations of bread making and dress making have started the campaign.[44]

Study plans and reading materials for the study clubs varied only slightly through the years. The social encyclicals and pertinent guild publications held first place in the topics under study. Some believed the materials were too elementary to provide sufficient challenge to maintain study club interest; others felt that as the war era approached, new materials, adapted to the needs of the times, were required. The striking revival of study club interest, and also of individual and school attention, close upon the publication of Father Crane's *Planned Social Study* in 1946 seemed to bear out the latter contention. Announcement of the work stated: "The Catholic Social Guild offers new and up-to-date study courses as a help to men and women of any age and of varying degrees of education and opportunity for study, who are interested in the social question."[45] And, indeed, the courses were so arranged as to be adaptable to individual, group, and school use. There was nothing haphazard about them; lessons, outlines, and readings were constructed on a weekly basis. Description in the prospectus ran as follows:

There are three types of courses offered. . . . They are known as A, B, and C courses. An A course is a short, beginner's course of six months. Our B course lasts nine months. It is the only course for which a Certificate may be gained and it must be taken as a prelude to the Di-

[44] XIX (August, 1939), 126–127.
[45] *Catholic Social Year Book, 1946*, p. 5.

ploma. C courses last nine months. Any two C courses must be taken along with a B course for the Diploma. At the moment we offer the following courses:

Course A (6 months) —The Nature of Man
Course B (9 months) —Social Ethics
Course C (9 months) —Man and Society
                        Moral Philosophy
                        International Order
                        Trade Unionism[46]

Holders of the certificate and diploma were given specific recognitions:

The holder of a Certificate in Social Ethics is recognized by Headquarters as possessed of the knowledge necessary to act as chairman to a study-circle studying that subject. Moreover, no one may qualify as a Guild indoor speaker on any subject unless he holds the Certificate. . . . The value of the Diploma lies in the fact that its holder is recognized by Headquarters as possessing the knowledge to chair a study group in *any* subject.[47]

The proliferation of study clubs seemed to herald an awakening that could well change the social world, but within a few years the enthusiasm declined. Father Crane attributed the loss of interest to a misunderstanding of the purpose of the study group, viz., that study was considered an end in itself rather than a means to an end. The guild secretary tersely stated his convictions:

It [the study group] has about it still . . . that air of Victorian "self-improvement" which is the relic of earlier days. . . . Let us bury the study group, understood as an end in itself, for good and all and let us substitute in its place the action group, made up of those who are striving at their place of work and elsewhere to set a Christian tone, establish a Christian lead and so return to the Guild's original idea of what a study group should be. Those

---

[46] *Ibid.*
[47] *Ibid.*

engaged in this kind of activity . . . need to study in order to act effectively; they need to meet in order to plan. For these, the action group is ideal; it gives them the knowledge, the companionship and so the strength which they must have if they are to act effectively for the establishment of the Kingdom of God.[48]

In accord with Father Crane's idea, action groups were initiated and in October, 1954, the Action Group Service was inaugurated. Use of the service was optional; it was a response to the general complaint of insufficient help and direction from the guild headquarters. Almost all of the groups utilized the weekly service. It provided the whole system and plan of study, and directed the individual's action. Father Crane had minutely prescribed the procedure of an action group in its use of the service. His explanation of, and recommendations for, the use of the action Group Service follows:

(a) *A Gospel Enquiry* whose essential object is to bring members of the Group into touch with the Person of Christ Our Lord. This is done by taking a short passage from the Gospels and using on it the See, Judge, Act method—seeing what is done, judging its significance and deciding how, in its light, one should act in the circumstances of one's daily life. Clearly, the service of a chaplain would be of the greatest help in this connection. All members of the Group should study before the meeting the passage of the New Testament selected for the Gospel Enquiry; and all should have a copy of the Knox version of the New Testament. The member of the group who is to lead the discussion on the Gospel Enquiry should try, if possible to see the Chaplain of the Group or a priest beforehand. If not, let him do the best he can. The Gospel Enquiry should not exceed fifteen minutes of the meeting's time. It is the business of the Chairman to see that it doesn't.

(b) *An Easy Outline* of Catholic Social Teaching, which

---

[48] Paul Crane, "Guild and College," *The Christian Democrat,* new ser., V (July–August, 1954) , 413.

is set out each time clearly and simply. These EASY OUTLINES will bet set out each time so as to make one complete and systematic whole. One member of the Group (a different one each time) should study this outline before the meeting, master its contents and then, *in his own way and without reading or referring to the outline,* lead the discussion on the point it contains. He should take no more than ten and no less than five minutes on this. After this there should be a short discussion, at the end of which the member who led the discussion, should read the EASY OUTLINE to the Group. The whole of this period (including every item) should not take longer than twenty minutes.

(c) *News Angle* which, each week, will take a significant item of news and treat it from a Catholic angle. It should be treated in *exactly* the same way and for *exactly* the same period of time as the previous item. Obviously, another speaker should lead the discussion on this item.

(d) *Reporting:* It remains to spend twenty minutes with each member of the Group reporting on progress made and difficulties encountered during the past week's effort at Social Action. When all have reported very briefly, there should be a brief discussion. It is important to notice under this head, that if no one has anything to report, they are obviously not active. After a time with nothing to report, it might be worth asking them what they are doing in the Group. The last two minutes of the twenty under this head should be spent by the Secretary reading the minutes of the last meeting.

The formal meeting of an Action Group should *always* close after one and a quarter hours *at the very most.* . . . The meeting should close with a decade of the Rosary, after which all should be free to go. Clearly, those who want to stay on to discuss can do so. It is recommended that the number in a Group should not exceed nine. It is recommended that meetings should be held each week; that the Chairman should exercise the firmest possible control over the time devoted to each item of the Meeting.[49]

---

[49] "Guild and College," *The Christian Democrat,* new ser., VI (February, 1955) , 111–112.

Beginners' enthusiasm gave the action groups an initial success, and in March, 1955, Father Crane commended the members: "It is good to be able to say that . . . the action groups are showing themselves more and more worthy of their name. Not only is their number growing, but the groups themselves are showing plenty of life."[50] Within two years, however, the tribute on vivacity changed to threnody on inertia:

> . . . I am somewhat disappointed with the great bulk of the Guild's Action Groups. . . .
> I would be less than honest if I gave any other as my opinion with regard to the Guild's Action Groups at the moment. Their zeal seems to me to be at low ebb. It will not be restored by . . . peregrinating priests from Guild Headquarters. The three things needed by most Action Groups at the moment are clear-sightedness, imagination and patient resolution.[51]

Like other areas of the guild's work, the study club movement was affected by the disruptive influences at work within the Catholic Social Guild during the 1950's. However, J. M. Cleary equated the situation with that of the Workers' Educational Association, which had also fallen prey to a general apathy.[52]

General Policies. In attempting to fulfill its basic aim of propagating Catholic social principles, the Catholic Social Guild, as a general policy, fostered every educative means and cooperated with every project and organization through which it could exert an influence on society. Week-end schools and day schools became prominent, and the attendance was always high. They were conducted at seminaries also, indicating the necessity for the clergy to be familiar with the social ques-

---

[50] "Guild and College," *ibid.,* 191.

[51] Paul Crane, "Current Comment," *The Christian Democrat,* new ser., VIII (July–August, 1957) , 403–404.

[52] *Op. cit.,* p. 212.

tion and the Church's teaching relating to it. In some areas colleges of social study were instituted. One such was opened in Manchester in 1937 with an enrollment of a hundred students. The courses offered were moral philosophy, apologetics, liturgy and plainsong, economics, and Catholic social doctrine. This venture was short-lived because of the war. Two years later a school of Catholic social studies was opened in London. Its initial curriculum comprised moral philosophy, Church history, Christian citizenship, and social history. In other areas courses were arranged in conjunction with the Workers' Educational Association, which entitled qualified lecturers to a grant in the form of payment for their services. Not infrequently lecturers in W.E.A. courses were former students of the Catholic Workers' College.

Co-operation of other Catholic societies was continuously sought by the Catholic Social Guild, and was generously and mutually given. Organizations regularly cited for collaboration in endeavors to permeate society with Catholic principles included the Catholic Young Men's Society, the Sword of the Spirit, the Catholic Truth Society, the Catenian Association, the Knights of St. Columba, the Catholic Women's League, and the Young Christian Workers. The Catholic Social Guild often had representatives in other organizations, such as Father Langdale on the National Catholic Youth Association and Dr. Fairfield in the "deliberations arranged by the Catholic Pharmaceutical Guild in order . . . to deal with the problem of race suicide and limitation of the family."[53] In 1945, in addition to the foregoing and other Catholic societies, lecturers on the Catholic Social Guild roster spoke under the auspices of the "university Catholic societies of Birmingham, Bristol, Edinburgh, Liverpool, Manchester, Reading and Southampton. . . . They have given talks at inter-

[53] "Report of the Thirty-third Annual Meeting, Catholic Social Guild" (August 2, 1942) , 4–5.

denominational gatherings and to groups in the Forces and Government hotels."[54] Indeed, the Catholic Social Guild tried "to make use of any help that may be available and to place our own services at the disposal of others."[55]

From the beginning the Catholic Social Guild was keenly aware of the need to deepen the spiritual life of the people if the social apostolate were to succeed. Hence, Father Plater inaugurated workingmen's retreats. After World War I and until 1939 these were conducted at the house of the religious of the Retreat of the Sacred Heart in Birmingham. Father Plater realized the good accomplished and wrote in 1920:

> This retreat house is working wonders, and figures can give little idea of its progress. It is sanctifying souls and giving to thousands of people a new appreciation of their faith and a genuinely apostolic spirit. It is bringing Catholics from the different parishes together to deepen their religious spirit and to encourage one another.[56]

In the first fifteen years retreats were given to upwards of 9,000 persons. Whenever and wherever accommodations could be found and arrangements could be made, retreats for workingmen were given at intervals. It is significant that in years of Catholic Social Guild decline, retreat attendance fell markedly.

Practical Program. In following its general policy, the Catholic Social Guild drew much criticism from those who felt that it was offering theory only—principles but no practical program stemming from them. In the year preceding the founding of the guild, Father Plater had written: "Had we a well-thought-out social programme, had we a Catholic Social

---

[54] "Report of the Thirty-sixth Annual Meeting, Catholic Social Guild" (July 29, 1945), 2.

[55] "Notes and Comments," *The Christian Democrat,* XVII (January, 1937), 2.

[56] Quoted in "Retreats," *Catholic Social Year Book, 1928,* p. 51.

platform transcending our differences of party politics, we might do much even with our small numbers to influence the social movements of the day."[57] But a year later, just prior to drawing up the statutes of the Catholic Social Guild, he had published an article entitled "A Catholic Society for Social Study,"[58] which embodied all the main policies and tenets along which the guild developed. It contained no plan of reorganizing the social order—only plans for teaching and permeating society with Catholic social principles. To these the guild adhered despite opposition from within as well as from without.

In 1912, Bishop Keating of Northampton, who had acted in an advisory and protective capacity in the early days of the guild,[59] and who was later to become its president, proclaimed a six-point program of social reform for the guild: (1) the living wage, (2) housing, (3) mutual help, (4) poor-law reform, (5) child hygiene, (6) fuller education. In 1921, with the launching of *The Christian Democrat,* the guild, as stated above,[60] declared a "social platform." Nevertheless, the demand for action reported by Henry Somerville as early as 1913 was not fulfilled. Tom Leyland continually encountered the demand for action on his tours, and in 1925, in his report as Organizing Secretary, he stated:

> Some attempt must be made to put our principles to the test. I find that the possibility of framing a programme, or a policy of social reform, is being eagerly discussed by many of our social sudents. . . . If we are to give a lead in social reform we shall need to do more than point out milestones: we must be prepared to mark out the route

[57] Quoted in Cleary, *op. cit.,* p. 34.

[58] *Ibid.,* pp. 36–37.

[59] It was Bishop Keating who defended the Guild against the accusation of being socialistic, and declared his willingness "to throw over the alleged redness of the C.S.G. a nice shade of episcopal purple" (Quoted in Cleary, *op. cit.,* p. 80).

[60] See p. ——

104

as well. It appears futile to insist on the right to a living wage and to a decent home, unless we are prepared to support and advocate measures which will make the attainment of these objects possible.[61]

Father O'Hea's reply, and that of the executive, was to reaffirm the guild's position as an educational body and its policy of avoiding party politics. The guild aimed to equip others for action—study club members who had learned the basic principles were to translate them into action in their places of employment, in local and national government, and in social work organizations.

In the mid-thirties the protestations against the lack of an action program resulted in the inauguration of a new publication, *The Catholic Worker,* by a group of guild members. Among them were Father Paul Crane, S.J.; Father John Fitzsimons; John Ford, the first editor; and Robert Walsh, editor at the paper's demise in 1959. At that time, as J. M. Cleary states, "by a neat reversal of circumstances he became editor of *The Christian Democrat* and organizing secretary of the Guild."[62] Some advocates of an action program argued that it was the place of the Catholic Social Guild to formulate the plan on which the Guild Social Order recommended by Pius XI in *Quadragesimo Anno* could be actualized in England.[63] Others acquiesced in Father O'Hea's adamant stand on the guild's educative policy but felt that the organization was out of touch with reality, that its teaching of Catholic social principles was in the abstract rather than in reference to the actual conditions, and therefore offered no solutions to social problems. An alternative to the action program was therefore suggested which would acquaint guild members and readers of guild publications with the problems and situa-

---

[61] Quoted in Cleary, *op. cit.,* pp. 101–102.

[62] *Ibid.,* p. 173.

[63] "Social Principles and Practice," *The Christian Democrat,* XIII (February, 1933), 26–29.

tions to which the principles should be applied. This program would have entailed a series of research projects and surveys to collect data and facts to form a profile of the social and economic conditions of England. Advocates of this program were convinced of the merits of this program as voiced by their spokesman:

> I believe whole-heartedly, that the members of the Guild and those other Catholics who, without being members, are yet alive to the urgency of the social problems of today, can contribute valuable assistance towards their solution, if they will arm themselves with a knowledge of actual conditions. That is why I want to see a survey undertaken; a survey carefully and truthfully documented and analysed according to the principles of the Encyclicals. I want the survey to be an accurate account of contemporary life, not of one section of it; and I want it to take into account justice as well as injustice; the happiness and contentment as well as the misery and discontent of our times.[64]

The response of the Catholic Social Guild under Father O'Hea's direction remained relatively unchanged through the years. Repeatedly the policies were set forth in *The Christian Democrat*:

> Let's be clear about aims: first to get the principles of our Faith to bear on matters of our own week-day lives, to lay a foundation of positive principle which will stand in good stead for ourselves and others in all sorts of unforeseen problems that may turn up, to get some grasp of the main principles of justice . . . not a collection of isolated principles, still less a "programme," but a philosophy founded on common sense. . . . Principles should give anchorage in storm and a driving force for progress.[65]

[64] M. B. Willison, "A Programme?," *The Christian Democrat*, XVII (December, 1937), 189–190.
[65]"Study Club News," *The Christian Democrat*, XVII (October, 1938), 158.

The C.S.G. has never been able to tell its members what to do and what to think in regard to every problem. . . . Rather, general C.S.G. policy has inevitably been so to train its members, through literature and study clubs, that each will have a reasoned grasp of principles and be able thus to convince and guide others . . . in all emergencies and occasions of daily life; . . .[66]

The Guild's function is primarily that of a teaching and learning body. It must endeavour so to train its members that they may generally be trusted to form right judgements and to promote wise action.[67]

This social education, whether with business men, working men or students, cannot profess to tell what each must do or think in every circumstance. . . . The aim is to create a spirit of loyalty to the Church and to lay foundations which will enable a man to stand on his own feet and arrive at sound conclusions.[68]

Such reiterations may have implied a *status quo* or unprogressive attitude, yet, as we have seen,[69] the guild modified its aims to meet the demands of the changed conditions of the war and postwar years. Nevertheless, Barbara Ward saw the guild as *the* organization to meet the challenge which the war presented—not with new aims and means but with new vigor in carrying out its policy of teaching: "And how are they to get that knowledge if the Guild resigns its office of spreading Catholic social principles, of preaching 'in season and out of season,' of exhorting and persuading, of 'compelling them to come in'? . . ."[70] Here, too, were evident the divergent opin-

[66] "Christian Truth in a New World Order," *The Christian Democrat,* XXI (February, 1941), 21–22.

[67] "What the C.S.G. Is For," *The Christian Democrat,* XXII (May, 1942), 41.

[68] Leo O'Hea, "The C.S.G.," *Sword of the Spirit,* Bulletin No. 59 (July 8, 1943), 7.

[69] *Supra,* p. 86.

[70] "The Challenge to the Guild," *The Christian Democrat,* XIX (November, 1939), 168.

ions which were to bring the Catholic Social Guild to a cross-roads in the late fifties. The middle of the decade saw the change from study clubs to action groups. Concurrently there was presented for discussion at the annual general meeting of 1955 a "programme of basic practical reform, according to Catholic social teaching,"[71] as resolved at the meeting of 1953. The announcement of the discussion as part of the summer school agenda stated:

> We feel it is time we turned our attention to the problem of social apostolate, the possibility of pointing it round a programme and what you might call the technique of its pursuit. To this end we are in process of collecting together a most capable panel of lecturers which includes already Professor Michael Fogarty, . . . Mr. Hamish Fraser, . . . and Miss M. D. Leys, . . .[72]

The program for social action, when completed, was really the work of Michael Fogarty and was published as the *Catholic Social Year Book, 1957*. In face of the dichotomy of views within the Catholic Social Guild at the time, the author's comments in the Foreword are significant:

> The Guild is a movement for education and discussion, and traditionally does not as a body adopt any policy. The views published here are therefore mine, not the Guild's. So far as the Guild is concerned, they are a contribution to discussion on the lines called for in 1953, but commit no one but myself.
>
> The 1953 resolution called for a programme for action now, not a general review of Catholic social doctrine. Therefore many points which might have been relevant twenty years ago, or which might become relevant some time in the future, have not been mentioned. Also this is

---

[71] Cleary, *op. cit.*, p. 219.

[72] "C.S.G. Summer School, Social Action: The Layman's Part," *The Christian Democrat*, new ser., VI (April, 1955), inside front cover.

a programme for the Catholic Social Guild, not for Catholic social action in general.

The program is comprehensive, covering the broad areas of (1) the special problems of our time, (2) the family and its neighbors, (3) working life, (4) world affairs, and (5) the organization of Catholic action. Disruption in, and reorganization of, the Catholic Social Guild have hampered and delayed implementation of the program, but it is noteworthy. J. M. Cleary paid tribute to it in his statement: ". . . were it to be studied and acted upon throughout the Catholic community, the next twenty years would see a revolution in that body and in the community of the realm comparable to anything that the first half of this century has witnessed."[73]

Specialized Organizations

There were various other organizations working with the Catholic Social Guild in the Social Catholic movement. Some of these were specialized; that is, they had specific areas in which they functioned, and/or membership was restricted to a particular group. The role of these representative organizations in trying to create a force that would leaven society with Catholic social principles merits consideration.

Employers' Associations. In *Christian Democracy in Western Europe, 1820–1953,* Michael P. Fogarty noted:

. . . British Catholic employers' associations emerged about or just after the Second World War; the British indeed enjoying the luxury of two, a Catholic Industrialists' Conference, which is officially recognized by the Catholic Employers' International, and an Association of Catholic Managers and Employers. All these are primarily educational organizations, concerned with such things as management training or the promotion of human relations in industry.[74]

[73] *Op. cit.,* p. 219.
[74] p. 256.

Beginning in 1937, the Catholic Industrialists' Conference has met twice annually. This was arranged particularly by the Catenians, under the auspices of the Catholic Social Guild. Catholic professionals and businessmen made up the membership of the Catenian Association, which promoted social intercourse among their group, furthered their interests through individual and collective action, and performed many works of benevolence for its members and their families in need.[75] A number of Catenians were members of the Catholic Social Guild, and it was largely their interest in the spread of Catholic social principles which aided in bringing about the bi-annual meetings. It was an attempt to fulfill the recommendations of Pius XI that "the Apostles of the industrial and commercial world should themselves be employers and merchants."[76]

The purpose of the gatherings was educative—to discuss social and economic problems in the light of Catholic principles and to plan their practical application. Attendance was generally small, but the work and study was very intense. At a typical week-end meeting, five discussion periods were usually held from Saturday evening until Sunday night. An outline of the topic under consideration was presented—frequently by Father Lewis Watt, S.J.—and the members did the rest of the work, analyzing the problems and drawing practical conclusions. The scope of the discussions can be ascertained from the report of the areas covered at a characteristic meeting:

> The general subject of the last meeting was Industry after the War and this covered such matters as self-government in industry, the guild social order, joint industrial councils and the force to be given to their decisions; the probable results of war-time monopoly, the question of recovery

---

[75] *Catholic Social Year Book, 1921,* p. 73.
[76] Husslein, *op. cit.,* p. 231.

from the concentration of industry; the future regulation of competition, of investment and capital expenditure, the effect of capital policy on the displacement of labour; family allowances.[77]

The Catholic Industrialists' Conference has continued to meet and to work quietly and unobtrusively, as Mr. George McClelland, Chairman of the conference, stated,

> to provide a meeting-place and forum for Catholic employers and higher executive management at the appropriate level, so that they could meet in a Catholic atmosphere, discuss their various problems and experiences to mutual advantage, and at the same time measure the results of these experiences against Catholic social principles and accepted moral codes and obligations.[78]

It was also important that the employer meet with the employee for joint consultation on problems which concerned both. The opportunity for such communication was realized by the formation of the Catholic Industrial Council, comprising Catholic trade unionists and employers in industry. Its inaugural meeting convened at Manchester in October, 1943, under the auspices of the Catholic Social Guild.[79] Unfortunately, this venture did not have the relative success and persistence of the conference.

The second organization, the Association of Catholic Managers and Employers, mentioned by Mr. Fogarty, also had its beginning under the auspices of the Catholic Social Guild and the initiative of the Catenians. Its germinal meeting was held in March, 1938, and while World War II interfered with the plan for more frequent conferences, a group did convene annually. Again, it was Father Lewis Watt, S.J., who repeated-

---

[77] "Notes and Comments," *The Christian Democrat,* XXI (June, 1941), 85.

[78] Cleary, *op. cit.,* p. 149.

[79] "Notes and News," *The Christian Democrat,* XXIII (December, 1943), 88.

ly presided and directed the discussions, which covered a wide range of topics: employers' associations, trade unions, and their mutual relations; labor management; and experiences of state control. These annual meetings preceded the recommendations of the hierarchy of England and Wales for the establishment of diocesan associations of Catholic managers and employers, as planned at the Low Week Meeting of 1948. Cardinal Griffin addressed the inaugural meeting of the Westminster Diocesan Association, and set forth the aims:

> . . . to assist and encourage all Catholic employers to join their appropriate Employers' Associations or Confederations where such exist, and to take an active and personal interest in the work of their own Association; secondly, to safeguard the interests of Catholics in such Confederations and to organize all Catholic employers in the dioceses in the Association. . . . Finally, to assist employers to inform themselves of the social principles of the Church and enable them to promote such principles and to defend them when assailed.[80]

Major Poole, chairman of the association, considered it "complimentary to the Workers' Apostolate, for we are both working to the same end; and as each grows in stature, so will they be brought ever closer together, for they have a common bond which no earthly power or coercion can sever."[81] Membership in the associations remained slight, but their efforts at studying and applying Catholic social principles, coupled with the work of employers, managers, and businessmen in the Sword of the Spirit, the Newman Society, and various professional guilds[82] could readily refute the accusation that this

---

[80] Cardinal Griffin, "Catholic Employers and Workers," *The Tablet,* CXCI (June 19, 1948), 390.

[81] Quoted in T. Cummins, "Any Questions ," *The Christian Democrat,* new ser., VI (April, 1955), 240.

[82] There were a number of guilds even before World War II, such as the Lawyers' Guild, or Society of Our Lady of Good Counsel,

class was doing nothing in the Social Catholic movement.

Catholic Parents' Association. A more general type of organization was the Catholic Parents' Association. In August, 1943, the Catholic hierarchy of England and Wales issued the following statement:

> The Hierarchy have given full approval to the formation of parochial and diocesan associations of Catholic parents, under the direction of the Bishops of the various dioceses, but they do not approve the formation of the National Federation of Catholic Parents' Associations, nor of its appeal for funds.[83]

The first of the associations was founded in the diocese of Brentwood, at Ilford, April 8, 1940. Other parishes and dioceses followed, but the great proliferation of the associations took place after the hierarchical approval. There were slight variations in the organization from diocese to diocese. Some preferred the longer title of Catholic Parents' and Electors' Association; the constitutions often varied, and the aims, too,

---

which gave legal aid absolutely free to poor persons, and the Doctors' Guild, or Guild of Saints Luke, Cosmas and Damian, which also addressed itself to care of the poor. However, the movement grew, and in September, 1956, Cardinal Griffin observed: "There is now a guild for almost every sphere of activity. We have guilds for Catholic artists and craftsmen, for civil servants, for actors, for men engaged in radio and in the Press, guilds for printers, social workers, doctors, nurses, and chemists. And many more besides. The object of all this has been two-fold: first, to train the members to be better Catholics, and second, to train the Catholics to be better professional men and women. By their regular meetings these guilds can do a great deal to strengthen and train the individual Catholic to take the faith into his own professional sphere.

"I am convinced that this development in the field of the lay apostolate has been one of the most significant in the development of the Church in this country during the post-war years" ("Out of the Catacombs," *The Tablet,* CCVIII [September 22, 1956], 221.

[83] "The Catholic Parents' Associations," *The Tablet,* CLXXXII (August 28, 1943), 104.

showed some divergence. In general, however, the objects of the associations were similar to those formulated by the groups in the Southwark diocese:

(1) To promote and safeguard Catholic interests generally and with special regard to the needs of Catholic Education; (2) To acquaint parents with their rights, duties, and powers; (3) To give attention to needs of Catholic Youth; (4) To promote and encourage representation on all public and educational bodies.[84]

It is significant that education held first place in the aims, for local problems regarding it frequently constituted the motivating force in the formation of an association. Whenever the education question became a national issue, there was great activity, and much energy was displayed to influence elections along lines favorable to Catholic education. J. D. Stewart in his study of pressure groups recognized the persuasive power of the associations:

The Roman Catholic Church (or to be more precise, Catholic Parents' and Electors' Associations) has been an active campaigner at elections on the issue of financial support for Catholic schools, hardly counterbalanced by the leaflets circularized by the Secular Education League or even the more formidable intervention of local Free Church Federal Councils, for the simple reason that the latter bodies do not command votes whereas it is considered that the Roman Catholic Church may. These tactics are remarkable in that it is probably the only group which places most weight during a campaign on election activities. If a group's role in an election is regarded as important, then its intervention therein may have as great an effect as months of routine campaigning.[85]

The immediate concern for several years was the education

[84] "Catholic Parents of the Southwark Diocese," *The Tablet,* CLXXXII (September 4, 1943), 119.
[85] *British Pressure Groups* (Oxfords: Clarendon Press, 1958, p. 229.

question, but the associations were intended to cope with other problems, and, in the words of one commentator, "the core of the long-term policy may well prove to be the preservation of family freedom, of the integrity of the family and of basic family rights."[86]

Structurally the organization was parochial, with central councils covering parliamentary divisions. There were diocesan councils also, and these in turn were represented in an inter-diocesan council of the Catholic Parents' and Electors' Association. In October, 1954, the hierarchy appointed the Bishop of Brentwood as ecclesiastical advisor to this body. Thus, while the idea of a national council did not receive episcopal approval, the prodigious spread of the associations had developed into a nation-wide organization.

The success of the movement has been attributed to

(a) a realization of the injustices in the White Paper (on education) ; (b) the lengthy preparation and experimentation for three and a half years by the laity in various parishes; (c) its essentially lay character; (d) the insistence on the system of elective representation of parents, on committees in parishes, by parents, for parents; and (e) the visible need for an expression by parents of their attitude to matters of basic family rights.[87]

These characteristics contain the earmarks of Catholic action organizations, and as such the Catholic Parents' associations functioned. The Bishop of Hexham and Newcastle spoke of the practical work of the organization as "Catholic Action of the purest water."[88] To fulfill its aims it was recognized that every "member must learn to be an apostle; . . ."[89] Individu-

---

[86] "The Catholic Parents' Movement," *The Tablet,* CLXXXII (November 27, 1943), 260.

[87] *Ibid.,* 259.

[88] *Ibid.,* 260.

[89] C. J. Woollen, "Parents' Associations in England," *Blackfriars,* XXV (August, 1944) , 295.

ally, within its ranks, and in conjunction with other organizations[90] the Catholic Parents' and Electors' Associations carried on their work—sometimes overtly in campaigns and the like, and at other times unobtrusively—in the Social Catholic movement.

Catholic Women's League. The *Catholic Social Year Book, 1921* ranks the Catholic Women's League as an organization for general purposes; with its restricted membership, however, it has a place in the organizations presently under consideration. *The Catholic Social Year Book, 1927* lists the organization with "National Charitable Associations," but its aim— "To unite Catholic women in a national society for the promotion of religious and intellectual interests and social work,"[91]—implied activities that involved it directly in the Social Catholic movement. In *The New Catholic Dictionary* its aims are extended to "ensuring the representation of Catholic interests on public bodies; and for the formation and collective expression of Catholic opinion."[92] Internationally, it was part of an organization "designed to place the organized energies of Catholic women at the service of the Church, for the defense of Catholic principles."[93]

Although the Catholic Women's League has had original enterprises, it has stood ready always to undertake any work or project that ecclesiastical authority might request, either on a temporary basis or as a permanent activity. Consequent-

[90] For instance: In 1955, with the Catholic Education Council it sponsored a conference for Catholic councillors "to bring to the attention of the members certain administrative and financial problems, present and future, facing Catholic schools, and to learn from Catholic Councillors their own difficulties and the suggestions they had to make" ("Catholics in Local Government," *The Tablet,* CCVI [November 12, 1955], 490).

[91] *Catholic Social Year Book, 1927,* p. 4.

[92] "Catholic Women's League," p. 184.

[93] *Ibid.,* p. 185.

ly, its efforts have reached over a wide range of interests, such as infant welfare, girls' clubs and hotels, and soldiers' recreation huts and canteens at home and abroad; it participated in the Guild of Women in Business and in the Union of Catholic Mothers; it had its own emigration committee in the Catholic Emigration Society; it formed the Association of Our Lady's Catechists and collaborated with the Catholic Social Guild in various ways.

In its concern for the preservation of the faith, particularly among the young, the league undertook various works, two of which were especially prominent. During the decade following World War I, when emigration of Catholic women and girls reached an unprecedented level, the Catholic Women's League evolved an elaborate machinery to protect, direct, and care for the emigrant, from planning the voyage to settling in the new country. It "links up with over fifty similar Catholic Women's leagues in all countries of the world,"[94] thus ensuring that the individual would be able to practice her religion in favorable circumstances. Its second important work in trying to stem the "leakage" from the Church was that of catechizing. The Association of Our Lady's Catechists "was formed in obedience to the desire of H. E. Cardinal Bourne that some organized lay help might be provided, in crowded parishes, or in those remote from a Catholic church and school, where the clergy need assistance in teaching the Faith to children."[95] Training centers were established, usually conducted by religious women, and Father F. C. Devas, S.J., was appointed Spiritual Director of the association. In 1928 a correspondence course was initiated, and the course was also given to the older girls in convent schools. By 1930

[94] Mrs. H. Taylor, "Catholic Emigration for Women and Girls," *The Christian Democrat,* IX (March 3, 1929), 44.

[95] Susan Cunnington, "Our Lady's Catechists," *The Tablet,* CLVII (March 21, 1931), 386.

117

there were 199 qualified catechists, and 120 were enrolled in the training courses. Despite such developments their numbers were insufficient to meet the requests from the clergy for their assistance.

The social service work of the Catholic Women's League penetrated every area, and helped to make members acutely aware of the social and economic conditions in England. This led to an active share in the Social Catholic movement on its own initiative and in collaboration with the Catholic Social Guild. Margaret Fletcher, founder of the Catholic Women's League, was also one of the founders of the Catholic Social Guild and served on its executive; she was also the great advocate and patroness of women students at the Catholic Workers' College. Under her direction, and subsequently, social problems were well to the fore in the program of the Catholic Women's League. The periodical, *The Crucible,* which she had launched, was "devoted to the enlightenment of Catholics on social questions."[96] The organization was founded on an all-class basis, so that every stratum of society was influenced by its projects and resolutions. All members were expected to participate in its undertakings. One of its most significant works was its study and recommendations in regard to the housing questions. Throughout England its members formed study clubs in affiliation with the Catholic Social Guild. This was due considerably to the urgings of Father O'Hea, S.J.; he perceived it as a means for all classes to learn in what way they could contribute something of value to the general good.[97]

In 1956 the Catholic Women's League celebrated its golden jubilee. During the fifty years its membership had grown from 14 to 22,000. It has constituted a force whose voice could

[96]"From Our Notebook," *The Tablet,* CCVII (June 9, 1956) , 542.
[97] "A Conference on Social Service," *The Tablet,* CLII (November 24, 1928) , 682.

be heard throughout the land, and statistical reckonings wil.
never adequately evince its accomplishments.

Catholic Evidence Guild. An organization specialized in
its aim but whose membership was open to clergy, laymen,
and laywomen, was the Catholic Evidence Guild. Its structure and objectives have been discussed previously,[98] and
while it was not directly concerned with the Social Catholic
movement, it is here considered for its role in dispelling
prejudice, in making Catholicism understood, and, therefore, in helping to make Catholic social principles acceptable.
The organization grew rapidly, but there were never enough
speakers for the work undertaken by the guild. Though it
unswervingly held to its policy of expounding doctrines and
practices of Catholicism only, there was controversy over the
refusal to teach Catholic social principles. One evidence guild
suggested that the Catholic Social Guild have its own open-
air lectures; another invited the Catholic Social Guild to
supply lecturers for Evidence Guild platforms.[99] Appreciating
the dangers that could accrue to the work of the Catholic
Evidence Guild, Henry Somerville, nevertheless, was of the
opinion that the social question should not be completely
ignored. He suggested that

> every Catholic Evidence speaker should have a certain
> amount of social knowledge, and some speakers would
> do well to specialise in the study of social subjects,
> particularly if they address meetings in industrial dis-
> tricts. . . .
> As a general rule Catholic Evidence lectures should not
> be specifically social lectures but social subjects should be
> treated only incidentally. . . . The Kingdom of Heaven
> is to be sought for its own sake, not because temporal
> things are added unto it.

[98] *Supra,* pp. 26-27.
[99] Henry Somerville, "Social Subjects and Catholic Evidence,"
The Christian Democrat, II (February, 1922), 7.

Catholic Evidence speakers . . . should send to *The Christian Democrat* questions they are asked on social subjects. An effort will be made to supply the best possible answers in these pages.[100]

Frank J. Sheed unequivocally stated that "the C.E.G. did not deal with social questions from the platform."[101] He contended that "social betterment was a vital need but, compared with the giving to the ordinary man a view of the supernatural, it was a purely secondary consideration."[102]

World War II brought a serious curtailment of Catholic Evidence Guild work, but it was quickly rejuvenated after the war. Actually, since the war, interest in the guild has been intensified and its membership has markedly increased. The following table portrays the widespread activity of the Catholic Evidence Guild shortly after the war.[103] The crowds, though more subdued, according to one opinion,[104] were interested. Maisie Ward and Frank J. Sheed contended that the quietness was indicative of an enervating spirit of indifference to religion, that the crowd was totally apathetic.[105] Walter Jewell stated that "no general need for new topics has been felt."[106] However, because of the change in attitude and religious ignorance, the topics had to be approached in a new way, from a new angle. The speaker of the postwar years had first to gain the interest of the audience. Proofs could no longer

---

[100] *Ibid.,* 8–9.

[101] "Catholic Evidence and Social Action," *The Christian Democrat,* VI (November, 1926), 169.

[102] *Ibid.*

[103] Information taken from Walter Jewell, "The Catholic Evidence Guild," *The Catholic Encyclopedia,* ed. Vincent C. Hopkins, S.J., XVIII, Supplement II (1958), n.p.

[104] *Ibid.*

[105] *Catholic Evidence Training Outlines,* 4th ed. (New York: Sheed & Ward, 1943), pp. 11–12.

[106] *Op. cit.,* n.p.

TABLE 2

1949 STATISTICS FOR C.E.G. IN ENGLAND

GUILDS	MEMBERS	EFFECTIVE SPEAKERS	MEETINGS PER WEEK
Archdiocese of Westminister			
Westminster	135	120	14
Archdiocese of Birmingham			
Birmingham	30	10	2
Potteries	10	6	2
Archdiocese of Liverpool			
Liverpool	40	20	4
Upholland Seminary	. . . .	6	. . . .
St. Helens	6	4	1
Diocese of Brentwood			
Forest Gate	24	10	2
Southend	19	5	2
Diocese of Hexham and Newcastle			
Newcastle	20	16	1
Diocese of Leeds			
Leeds	120	7	1
St. Michael's College	16	2	. . . .
Bradford	120	27	3
Diocese of Middleborough			
York	30	9	1
Diocese of Nottingham			
Nottingham	9	3	1
Derby	16	6	1
Leicester	23	12	1
Diocese of Salford			
Manchester	20	11	3
Diocese of Southwark			
Southwark	. . . .	28	9

be the focal point of a lecture; exposition of a doctrine constituted the major part of the teaching. This involved showing the riches of Catholicism implied in the doctrine, for the apathetic listener would scarcely have been moved by simple definition. That the guild met the challenge successfully is evident today.

Youth Associations

Catholic Young Men's Society. The Catholic Young Men's Society, perhaps the eldest of Catholic organizations in England, has had a continuous existence since 1849, when it was founded by Dean O'Brien. The title is somewhat misleading, for membership includes married men with families as well as the young, unmarried men whom the title more readily connotes. The simplicity of its rules—monthly Communion, exclusion of politics, and the power of veto for the chaplain of each branch—coupled with its purpose of personal spiritual, intellectual, and social well-being, have made it attractive to young men. In 1921 its membership was estimated at 21,000,[107] and in 1941 its 258 branches had an approximate total membership of 30,000.[108]

To fulfill its purpose the society provided a threefold program. For individual spiritual formation, rooted in the Church's doctrine of "corporateness," it proposed the practice of monthly corporate Communion for some intention of the parish, daily Mass, annual retreats, and family prayers. Intellectual development was fostered through the "annual Plan of Study which aims in action at reaching the actual living circumstances of each member."[109] Topics of study varied

---

[107] *Catholic Social Year Book, 1921,* p. 66.

[108] "Catholic Young Men's Society," *The Catholic Encyclopedia Dictionary* (New York: The Gilmary Society, 1941), p. 1031.

[109] Denis Hickling, "Where Catholic Societies Fail," *The Christian Democrat,* new ser., XII (March, 1961), 103.

annually—"Holy Mass," "Christ the Teacher," and "Christian Unity" are samples. A monthly bulletin was issued to present each section of the plan of study. Since the intellectual training was to have a practical application in life, it carried over into the social sphere of the threefold program. All branches provided recereational facilities and opportunities for members.

In 1921, at the Catholic Congress, objection was voiced to the meagerness of intellectually stimulating entertainment which would attract persons who sought diversions "above cards and billards."[110] Through the years this situation altered considerably. The branches entered into a variety of activities. They conducted study clubs and debating societies; established reading and literary circles, libraries, and savings banks; undertook aftercare of boys leaving school; arranged evening classes in cooperation with the local education authority; and provided business and social introductions for members who were traveling. Proof of the extended program was evidenced by the improved quality of membership, which previously had not included many men interested in intellectual pursuits or in public affairs. With considerable satisfaction, the society in 1961 claimed: ". . . we number among our members a great many Councillors, several Mayors and numerous active trade unionists. Our information service on T.U. affairs deals with every facet of Union life."[111] Activities on a national scale involved plans for meetings and lectures on specific subjects, e.g., Church and state; debate campaigns on current issues; and protest propaganda, against anything that contributed to the lowering of moral standards or the extension of materialism, e.g., indecent films.[112]

[110] *Catholic Social Year Book, 1921*, p. 21.
[111] Hickling, *op. cit.*, 103.
[112] T. W. C. Curd, "Catholic Inaction," *The Month*, CLXV (March, 1935), 270.

Basically, the Catholic Young Men's Society was parochial in structure and as such was completely "at the disposal of the parish priest for the work of the Church in his particular area."[113] It also functioned at the diocesan and national levels, so that it served as a unifying force within the Church. In some areas it cooperated with the Catholic Social Guild, and many study clubs of the society's members were conducted under the auspices of the guild. On the occasion of the Society's centenary, 250 members in Rome were given the Church's direct approbation through an address by the Holy Father, which included a commendation:

> The Church in England knows well how faithfully your society has carried out the purpose for which it was founded; how you have helped one another, by example and material encouragement, in the frequentation of the sacraments and in all the practices of your holy religion; how, in the sphere of social action, many of your branches have, by means of debates, discussions and study groups, helped to spread a true understanding of the Church's teaching on social questions, so that you may justly boast that you have been the faithful helpers of your clergy and Bishops.[114]

Young Christian Workers. The Catholic Social Guild claims to be the cradle of the Young Christian Workers in England, but the association has developed independently. Attention had first been drawn to it by articles in *The Christian Democrat.*[115] The initial leaders of the Y.C.W. in England were selected from a Catholic Social Guild study group

---

[113] Hickling, *op. cit.*, 103.

[114] "Pope Pius XII and the C.Y.M.S.," *The Tablet,* CXCIV (October 22, 1949), 270.

[115] Father O'Hea, S.J., had described the organization as it was developing in Belgium in 1928. In 1933, an article by George Lake, "How Jocistes Run Their Study Clubs," emphasized the tremendous vitality and practicality of the association.

made up of sellers of *The Catholic Worker*,[116] and the organization was officially established in February, 1937. At the first annual congress, December 4, 1937, membership stood at one hundred in six groups. A year later their strength had doubled, to eleven groups with two hundred members.[117] While this rate of increase did not continue annually, the organization did spread rapidly, and its zealous members could be found in every type of work.

The very challenge which the purpose of the Y.C.W. presents to youth constitutes the loadstone of its success. It assumes responsibility for every interest—spiritual, moral, intellectual, and social—of the young worker. The plan of action for which each member is trained is to "see the facts of the situation as they are, judge them in the light of Christ's teaching, and act upon them when and where necessary."[118] It is the "see, judge, act" method now familiar to all Catholic actionists. But this is not the whole of the program. Basic to the social activity is the self-formation that must take place. Every meeting has on its agenda a Gospel inquiry into some aspect of Christ's life. The attempt "to show forth the personality of Christ in everything they do"[119] is the ideal of the young workers. Finbar Synnott saw in the whole program the "apostolate of the worker—formation as well as defence of him. The Worker is the apostle of the Worker, in a man-to-man or boy-to-boy language he can understand."[120] Two years after its foundation the English conceded the efficacy of the Y.C.W. program:

---

[116] Cleary, *op. cit.*, p. 174, n.

[117] Finbar Synnott, "Progress of the Y.C.W.," *Blackfriars*, XIX (October, 1938), 762.

[118] Joseph Christie, "Compassion on the Multitude," *The Tablet*, CLXXXIX (June 28, 1947), 330.

[119] *Ibid.*, 331.

[120] *Op. cit.*, 763.

We can see now why it is that Pope Pius XI more than once insisted on the Young Christian Workers' Movement being an authentic form of Catholic Action. This movement is a means of restoring to the ranks of organized Labour the Church's social teaching, not so much by preaching as by practice, by *being* Catholic working men and women in accordance with the double aspect of right labour, labour directed to the immediate good of the community in its properly ordered aspect, and labour directed to the last end of man and of the society of which he forms part.[121]

An extensive part of the work of the Y.C.W. in England concerned the working boy or girl just before leaving school. Contact was established early, not only to prevent "leakage" but, from the positive view, to prepare the young worker, as Cardinal Griffin stated at a Y.C.W. rally, to cope with the "pagan surroundings" and to face the difficulties which "arise not so much from morals as from the terrible ignorance of your non-Catholic fellow-workers. . . . They probably have completely different ideas about religion, about home life and about marriage."[122] In this work of acclimatization a program was devised to

take him [the prospective worker] over whole—see that he gets a job with reasonable prospects and suited to him; defend his interests in it, (partly through Unions which all members are encouraged to join and Christianize); it will give him social services outside, saving schemes and sickness service and the like . . . it will bring him into a form of instruction where his life in its entirety worked out in terms of his faith, and its problems as so solved; it will give him an ideal of himself as an apostle and minister of direct social service to his friends. It will give him a pride in the status of worker for the sake of

[121] Michael de La Bedoyers, "Catholic Action and the Catholic Layman," *The Month* CLXXIV (September, 1939), 240.

[122] "The Young Christian Workers," *The Tablet*, CC (November 1, 1952), 366.

Christ. All will be centered around the Mass . . . it is going to bring him the strengthening of companionship and joy. . . .[123]

Through this program a co-organization developed—the Pre-Y.C.W. It was established in 1949 by Patrick Keegan, and within approximately two years it numbered 150 groups. It is modeled on the Y.C.W. itself, and members range in age from 13½ to 15½. Training of the boys and girls is undertaken in cooperation with parents, parish priests, teachers, and employment officers. The whole program is directed so that "the change-over from school to work and the general development of the early adolescent to the age when he can join a regular Y.C.W. group is as smooth as possible and gives the maximum opportunity for his development."[124] Like the Y.C.W., the Pre-Y.C.W. is not a purely religious body; it aims to develop the whole person and through his balanced adjustment to leaven the youth of society with Catholic thought and principles.

Clubs and Other Groups. There was a variety of other youth associations which flourished intermittently in England in the period 1920–1955. Awareness of the necessity for the guidance of youth, especially in the early teens, prompted the formation of clubs and associations. A twofold aim, viz., stemming the "leakage" and inculcating Catholic social principles, was common to the various groups.

Scouting was one of the most successful ventures in youth organization; there were troops for girls as well as for boys. It had been inaugurated by a non-Catholic, but troops very early become denominational and, as such, nation-wide. There were the Catholic Scout Council and the Catholic Scouts' Advisory Committee, including Catholic Girl Guides, "formed with the approval of the Hierarchy to co-ordinate organiza-

---

[123] Synnott, *op. cit.,* 763–764.
[124] John M. Todd, "Leaving School," *The Tablet,* CC (August 30, 1952), 167.

tion throughout the country and to assist the clergy in the formation and control of parochial troops."[125] Almost every diocese had a representative on the Catholic Scouts' Advisory Committee, while troops were formed on a parochial or district basis. During the 1920's the Catholic Women's League, on the request of Cardinal Bourne, participated in the Girl Guide movement. In 1929, however, the league resigned from the Girl Guides' Association and the work was coordinated with that of the Catholic Scouts' Advisory Committee.

Numerous girls' and boys' clubs existed in the parishes throughout England. Their titles and immediate purposes varied extensively, and compilation of complete and accurate information on them is scarcely possible. A commentary on the Catholic clubs of one city, Birmingham, indicates their vitality and significance, and emphasizes their selfless leadership:

> The Catholic clubs, some forty in number, form one of the largest units in the city, but by far the majority of them also belong to some specifically religious group, such as The Grail, The Young Christian Workers, the Junior Legion of Mary, the younger members of C.Y.M.S., and other societies. They put faith first and affiliation second. Yet, preferring, as a rule, to do without paid instructors, and receiving hardly a penny in grant aid, the Catholic group not only has its own priest organizer, but runs its own retreats and leadership courses, supports a Youth Hostel of its own, edits its own magazine and manages its own film unit, and drama, swimming and sports festivals. Yet all its work is subordinate to the larger whole, treating youth not as a separate unit but as an integral part of family, school and parish.[126]

[125] *Catholic Social Year Book, 1927,* p. 3.

[126] T. S. Copsey, "The Post-War Generation," *The Tablet,* CXCV (May 13, 1950), 377. The article is a criticism of the "Report on Youth in Birmingham," made by a Free Church group, which, though it gave special recognition to the Y.C.W., did not give an adequate appraisal of Catholic youth work on the whole.

As the World War II era approached, and the effects on the Continent of Mussolini's and Hitler's youth camps became more apparent, concern in England for its own youth became more intense. In 1938, the Youth Section of the Unions of Catholic Women was established in accordance with the wishes of the bishops. This Catholic action organization for girls, subject to the bishop in each diocese, comprised three branches:

The Young Christian Workers (Y.C.W.) for the working girls between the ages of fourteen and thirty in parishes.

The Young Christian Students (Y.C.S.) for the students in secondary schools and training colleges, from fourteen upwards.

The Young Christian Groups (Y.C.G.) for girls belonging to the professional or more leisured classes, aged between seventeen and thirty. This branch to be interparochial.[127]

A fourth branch, the Young Christian Forces (Y.C.F.), was initiated during the war. Each group functioned as did the Y.C.W.,[128] working among its kind—seeing, judging, acting—to meet the difficulties, to try to solve the problems of its own environment. The C.A.O.G. aimed "to build a new Youth leading a new life, with a new conception of work, love, of family life and of all society."[129]

To encourage young girls to join associations and to enter some field of social work, the Grail, at the request of Cardinal Hinsley, organized a Catholic action camp. It was a week devoted to discussion and study of the problems of the day, and the means by which youth could help to ameliorate conditions. Inspiration and motivation were given by representa-

[127] "The Catholic Action Organisation for Girls," *The Tablet*, CLXXII (July 30, 1938), 157.

[128] Discussed on p. ——

[129] Carmelita Creville, "Our Girls," *The Sword of the Spirit*, Bulletin No. 64 (December 2, 1943), 9.

tives of the Catholic Evidence Guild (Frank Sheed), the Liturgical movement (Dom Bernard McElligot, O.S.B., and Father Clifford Howell, S.J.), family life (Baroness Beaumort), the press (David Walker), the social question (Nancy Hugh-Smith), civic responsibility (Mrs. Councillor Kemball), the apostolate of the stage (Robert Speaight), the Young Christian groups (Brenda St. Lawrence), the Grail, the Legion of Mary, the Catholic Guides Advisory Council, and Catholic Action (the Hon. Henry Hope, President of the Westminster Board of Catholic Action).[130] This experimental camp was held in August, 1938; its success gave promise of others to follow. It was an indication of the earnestness in the endeavors to train youth for Catholic action and to maintain among youth a Christian spirit.

The seriousness of the problem of safeguarding youth was recognized by the government, and in 1940 it set up the National Youth Committee to advise the Board of Education in aiding the existing efforts and in expanding provisions for social and physical recreation for boys and girls of fourteen to twenty who had left school. Local youth committees were also set up "with the outstanding aim of securing the fullest possible co-operation between Local Education Authorities and voluntary organizations."[131] Thus the Catholic Scout troops, the Girl Guides, and various clubs were represented on the committees. There was also provision for "direct representations of religious denominations,"[132] so that clergymen could be committee members. The Catholic Social Guild advised active support of representatives and of those interested in youth, since "the method adopted stands for the important

---

[130] "First Catholic Action Camp in England," *The Tablet,* CLXXII (August 13, 1938), 218.

[131] "Notes and Comments," *The Christian Democrat,* XX (September, 1940), 131.

[132] *Ibid.*

principle of close collaboration between public authority and voluntary and religious bodies," and "far from suffering harm, our Catholic organizations should benefit greatly. . . ."[133] After a few months it was clear that the interest of the youth committees was predominantly recreational. While still urging cooperation, the Catholic Social Guild advocated that members assume educational leadership, for

> the need is for competent instruction to provide a grasp of the main elements of Catholic social doctrine and to cultivate the sense of loyalty to the Faith which comes by the revelation to the worker of the beauty and strength of the great social Encyclicals. All must be related . . . to the actual surroundings of the young wage-earner.[134]

Realizing the limitations of the work of the National Youth Committee and the local youth committees, the hierarchy of England and Wales in 1942 set up the National Catholic Youth Association, with Bishop Mathew as chairman. It was to represent the total Catholic effort in the field of youth work for boys and girls between fourteen and twenty, and it aimed "to ensure that Catholic interests are fully safeguarded in any official schemes for youth organizations, and to give immediate consideration to any problems affecting Catholics that may arise."[135] The controlling council, under the presidency of Cardinal Hinsley and the vice-presidency of the diocesan archbishops and bishops, was composed of "representatives of each of the dioceses and of each of the National Catholic Societies working in any *active*, as distinct from purely spiritual, way for Catholic Youth."[136] A succession of youth

---

[133] *Ibid.*

[134] "Notes and Comments," *The Christian Democrat,* XXI (February, 1941), 19.

[135] "A National Catholic Youth Association," *The Tablet,* CLXXIX (May 2, 1942), 218.

[136] *Ibid.*

meetings, rallies, and summer schools followed the establishment of the N.C.Y.A. Many of the gatherings centered attention on the joint pastoral letter of the hierarchy of 1942[137] to acquaint youth with the social question. From the pastoral letter youth could learn Catholic social principles, and through their organizations they could participate in the amelioration of conditions. Diocesan youth associations, like that of Westminster, were also initiated. At the latter's inaugural meeting Cardinal Hinsley stressed the association's purposes: "to promote the full Catholic formation of the rising generation," and "to counteract the wrong direction that might be given to the National movement."[138] As in many of the youth groups, enthusiasm and energy were characteristic, and an attendant at one of the meetings wrote appreciatively:

> It was a privilege and pleasure to be invited to a demonstration at the Stoll Theatre where Westminster Catholic Youth Association presented a "Charter of Youth," ably expounding to a crowded gathering of young people by six of themselves; evidence of hard work done by many and drawing many together in a forceful movement.[139]

While the youth associations continued to flourish, and their meetings and study weeks drew large numbers, they nevertheless had their critics. C. J. Woollen, though he saw the organizations as a means of restraining the "leakage," thought they needed a common, stabilizing interest. This, he suggested, should be the foreign missions. In such a way, youth could fulfill the ideal set by Pope Pius XI: "Every Catholic

---

137 "The Church at Home," *The Tablet,* CLXXX (September 19, 1942), 144.

138 "The Church at Home," *The Tablet,* CLXXX (December 26, 1942), 316.

139 "Study Club News," *The Christian Democrat,* XXIII (June–July, 1943), 48.

a missionary." To him, the missionary spirit was a panacea for youth problems:

> To become mission-minded is to become apostolic, and the making of each new missionary in spirit is to give to one more at least a direction which will solve the problem of the rival loyalties of an often deluded adolescence. It will give back the home, the starting-point of apostolicity and vocation, its proper place, and emphasise its priority. Thus will the Catholic Youth Movement become the solution of the leakage.[140]

Harsher terms were employed by another critic, who believed that the "Youth Movements are the modern invention of the devil. They are an unavoidable invention, following necessarily upon the devil's destruction of the family."[141] He viewed the emphasis on youth as creating a "class" of youth and as making of the country "a vast orphanage and in order to establish any order, the ten-year-olds, the seventeens, the twenty-ones must be bunched together in 'forms.' "[142] On such a foundation Hitler and Mussolini had built. The critic conceded that some youth organization might be necessary, but it was not to be "more than first-aid while the slower but real cure is begun."[143] In his opinion, "when youth is no longer a class but has been absorbed once again into family life it will cease to be a problem suggesting 'movements' as a solution. The responsibility of youth will be the responsibility of the Christian family."[144]

Obviously, this was viewing the Catholic youth movement from an extreme angle. While one purpose of the organiza-

---

[140] "A Solution of the Leakage," *Blackfriars,* XXVII (March, 1946), 99.

[141] "Christian Rejuvenation," *Blackfriars,* XXV (October, 1944), 364.

[142] *Ibid.*

[143] *Ibid.,* 365.

[144] *Ibid.*

tions was the salvation of youth, yet there was always the aim, too, of permeating all society with Catholic social principles, and the best apostle for youth was youth. The young were to be part of the Social Catholic Movement; age was to have no priority in Catholic action of any kind.

Diocesan Catholic Action Plan

In response to the repeated and expanded recommendations of Pope Pius XI for the organization of Catholic action, the Catholic hierarchy of England and Wales, in December, 1936, issued a joint pastoral letter, "The Apostolate of the Laity."[145] It pointed out the need for Catholic action in England and indicated the plans for implementing it. These were in harmony with the Church's directives on the organization of Catholic action, of which A. M. Crofts summarized the basic ideas:

> Catholic Action is hierarchical. So also must be its organization. Since it is entirely and completely an instrument in the hands of the hierarchy, its organizations . . . must be grouped around the body of the Bishops of the Church. . . . There must be liberty in, never independence, of that body. Only through the fulfilment of that condition will multiplicity of organizations achieve greater efficiency through variety of purpose and at the same time unity of action.[146]

The general program of Catholic action in England contained six points:

> (i) Each diocese is to appoint a Diocesan Board in accordance with its own requirements. (ii) The Diocesan Boards are to be co-ordinated by a National Board con-

---

[145] "Joint Pastoral Letter of the Hierarchy of England and Wales on 'The Apostolate of the Laity,' Advent, 1936," *The Tablet,* CLXVIII (December 19, 1936), 866.

[146] *Catholic Social Action* (London: Alexander Ouseley, Ltd., 1936), p. 233.

sisting of one representative from each of the four provinces. These representatives are to be appointed by an Executive Board of Bishops, consisting of the four Metropolitans with the Archbishop of Westminster as President, the Metropolitans consulting their respective suffragan bishops in the appointment of the representatives. The National Board may be enlarged with the approval of the Hierarchy. (iii) The base of the organization is to be parochial . . . although the respective bishops are to organize Catholic Action according to their own requirements. (iv) Both National and Diocesan Boards and Parochial Councils are to consist of laymen, with at least one ecclesiastical assistant. (v) All three organizations are to keep in view the main problems of these countries, as outlined in the Joint Pastoral, 1936: (a) The leakage problem; (b) The extension of the Faith; (c) The solution of the social problem. (vi) The Diocesan Councils and the National Board are to have power to invite existing societies to undertake special activities consonant with their constitutions, or to appoint Committees *ad hoc,* e.g., for the youth problems, the young Catholic workers, and for social and industrial questions.[147]

While the bishops were to plan the Catholic action strategy according to the needs of their respective dioceses, and at the same time it was to be basically parochial, certain principles had to be kept in mind. These were succinctly set forth by Henry Waterhouse, S.J., and are here briefly summarized: (1) Catholic action must embrace all persons; birth, age, class, or training may bar no one. (2) It converts and directs all participating associations into the social apostolate, without interference in their other policies. (3) It must be above party politics, but it must fit persons for public office and must leave open the wide field of action public life offers. (4) In its government there must be absolute submission to the bishops,

[147] "Catholic Action," *The Tablet,* CLXXI (February 19, 1938), 233.

who in turn will back it up. (5) Catholic action aims at personal perfection, but it is also an apostolate and is meant to draw into the Church those whom priests cannot reach.[148]

As the bishops worked to lay the groundwork for the type of Catholic action best suited to their local needs, two major procedures emerged, as illustrated by the dioceses of Westminster and Liverpool respectively. The former "preferred to hammer out in a certain amount of detail the full scheme so that everything, objects, methods and constitution, should be clear before the work began."[149] The latter "preferred to define the scheme in very broad outline and to leave the detail to be hammered out by action."[150] From time to time, the Board of Direction of Westminster Catholic Action issued statements of services available, e.g., a panel of voluntary speakers, both clergy and laymen, for central gatherings or for parochial lectures and debates.[151] It regularly issued circulars to keep parochial councils in touch with the board; to provide information, suggestions, and reports that would aid in parochial activity; and to allot specific tasks to the parochial council. It further suggested committees whose duties covered "the Spiritual Apostolate, the Church's Teaching, Census and Membership, Youth Welfare, Press and Vigilance, Social Activities, a Social Committee, and Administration of Finance."[152] Local initiative was considerably curtailed by such minute recommendations. Perhaps there were more errors in the Liverpool diocese, but the flexibility of the program "allowed it to seize opportunities that would have been

---

[148] "Catholic Action—Towards a Better Understanding," *The Christian Democrat,* XIV (March, 1934), 43.

[149] Robert P. Walsh, "Catholic Action in England," *The Ecclesiastical Review,* C. (March, 1939), 260.

[150] *Ibid.*

[151] "Catholic Action," *The Tablet,* CLXXII (April 22, 1939), 532.

[152] "Westminster Catholic Action," *The Tablet,* CLXXIII (May 13, 1939), 628.

missed if tied down by a rigid constitution."[153] While parochial councils dealt with smaller problems in their immediate
vicinity, they also participated in the more extensive programs
planned by the board, e.g., an attack on social injustices, "dealing with low wages, bad housing conditions, high rents, inadequate unemployment relief."[154] As early as March, 1938,
the Archbishop of Liverpool inaugurated a plan for a college
of Catholic action in the archdiocese. Its purpose was "the
production of a well-informed Catholic laity and the training
of apostles for Catholic Action."[155] Full courses of study were
to be offered, but it was also intended to establish week-end
schools, day schools, summer schools, and correspondence
courses, so as to make educational facilities available for all
classes of students and for as many as possible.

The enthusiastic beginnings of the diocesan Catholic action
programs were soon frustrated by the worsening war conditions, which prohibited many activities, and by the new and
multiplying problems occasioned by the war. At the same
time a new movement, the Sword of the Spirit (to be discussed in Chapter IV), usurped much of the enthusiasm. In
limited fashion many existing organizations carried on for the
duration of the war. The postwar years heard a cry for new
interest in the lay apostolate,[156] for a revival of the Social
Catholic movement. Some felt there should be a complete
reorganization, from the sectional system of association—i.e.,
from men, women, and youth, respectively—to a family-parish
basis.[157] Another opinion was that insufficient emphasis had

[153] Robert P. Walsh, "Catholic Action in England," p. 260.

[154] *Ibid.,* 264.

[155] "Liverpool College of Catholic Action," *The Tablet,* CLXXI
(March 19, 1938) , 380.

[156] The term "Catholic action" gave place to "lay apostolate" in
the years following the war and during the time of Pope Pius XII
("The Lay Apostolate," *The Tablet,* CCX [October 5, 1957], 275) .

[157] Stanley E. Norfolk, "The Parish As a Unit," *The Christian
Democrat,* new ser., II (February, 1951), 29–34.

been placed on the apostolate to which each individual Catholic was called; his obligation to become informed, and then articulate in defending and explaining Catholic social principles and religious beliefs and tenets.[158] Still others believed that the Liturgical movement would provide the answers to religious apathy as well as to the social question.[159] Finally, the overlapping, the proliferation, of organizations was held responsible for the lack of achievement in the Social Catholic movement; and amalgamation, with a centralized control and direction of all organizations, was advocated.[160]

The only real plan devised for a reconstruction of Catholic action was the "Programme for Social Action" drawn up by Michael P. Fogarty and published as the *Catholic Social Year Book, 1957*.[161] Though the "Programme" has not been tried, it merits attention, and Section V, "The Organization of Catholic Action," is here quoted in both outline and diagram.

22. Catholics, as in the past, to be trained for social action in Catholic Action movements, but to be expected to make their way in politics, or in the unions, or other neutral movements without the help of any Catholic pressure group. To promote more discussion and party or group formation within these neutral movements, but to avoid establishing Christian or Catholic pressure groups, or "front" organizations inspired by them.

23. To help to develop three main types of Catholic Ac-

[158] Paul Crane, S.J., "Challenge of Today," *The Christian Democrat,* new ser., IV (November, 1953), 241–244.

[159] Clifford Howell, S.J., "The True Christian Spirit," *The Christian Democrat,* new ser., V (February, 1954), 77–79; "Our Witness to Christ," *The Christian Democrat,* new ser., V (September–October, 1954), 465–467.

[160] C. L. McDermott, "There's a War On," *The Christian Democrat,* new ser., I (December, 1950), 274–278.

[161] *Supra,* pp. 108-109.

tion—the triangle of youth movement, family movement, and working life movement—with such bodies as the C.S.G. supplying central services to all three. To promote effective consultation between these movements.

24. To promote specialization by social class within each of these movements, but not separate class movements.

25. To make more use of social research (religious socio-ology movement), and of small specialist conferences on matters of current importance, . . . To make more provision for intelligence work on the activities as well as the ideas of the Catholic social movements at home and overseas.

26. To see that evidence is presented on behalf of the Catholic Social Movement at all relevant public enquiries, and statements put out on important current issues.

27. Even more than in the past, to make a wide and deep spiritual development a central part of training for Catholic social action. To promote consultation among different Catholic social movements on their programmes for this.

28. To relate study more closely to action, study of and training in the most effective forms of Catholic social action, as well as the study of aims and objectives as proposed under (25).

29. To promote a general increase in contributions to the Church, having in mind particularly the needs of central services such as those referred to under point (22). To take as an immediate target half-a-crown per earner per week in the Sunday collection.[162]

---

[162] *Catholic Social Year Book, 1957*, p. 11.

FIGURE 2
THE TRIANGLE OF CATHOLIC SOCIAL ACTION[163]
Youth Movement
[Y.C.W. as model]

Specialized service
organizations such as

Sword of the spirit
(international affairs)
C.S.G.
(social affairs)
Newman Survey
(social research)
Newman Association
(lecture etc. service)

Family movement
[C.F.M. as model]

—Family League
(neutral, family
trade union)
—Cana movement and
marriage guidance
—Neighbours
—Community associations,
other voluntary associations
—Local government
—Social services (including
housing and family allowances)
—Savings movement
etc.

Areas
influenced

Working Life movement
Service Committees,
industry and national
Councils, etc.

[163] Reproduced from *Catholic Social Year Book, 1957,* p. 143.

—Firms
—Trade unions
—Employers' asso-
    ciations, etc.

Fogarty realized the difficulties involved in putting the program into practice. The existing organizations, included in the plan, overlap in their activities; this should be remedied so that greater efficiency in specific areas may be achieved. Yet the groups cannot work in isolation or in absolute independence, for as the chart indicates, "the work of the youth, family, and working life movements, and of the specialized central services, interlocks all along the line."[164]

Besides the organizations considered here, there were various movements that, by participation or indirectly, influenced the Social Catholic movement. A study of their plans, experiments and accomplishments will give some indication of their relevant importance.

---

[164] *Ibid.*, p. 146.

Chapter IV

DEVELOPMENT AND PROGRESS OF VARIOUS MOVEMENTS

One of the many facets of the Social Catholic Movement in England, 1920–1955, was constituted of movements which endeavored to "renew the face of England," to restore a Christian economic and social system and spirit. The three outstanding movements of the period were Distributism, Back-to-the-Land, and the Sword of the Spirit. Each will be considered in the light of its contribution to the Social Catholic movement, which, as indicated previously, aimed to produce a leavening force that would permeate society and direct the political, economic, and social changes and developments along Christian principles.

Distributism

Leaders. Distributism[1] originated in the decade preceding the period of this study. It claimed to carry out the exhortation of Pope Leo XIII in *Rerum Novarum*: "The law, there-

---

[1] Hilaire Belloc seems to have been the first to use the phrase "the Distributive State." He thus designated a period between the ancient and modern capitalistic forms of the servile state. According to Belloc, in the Distributive State "there were more varied and better balanced forms of ownership. On estates and in the villages there were common lands and privately owned lands. Guilds held in common only the property necessary to their cooperative life. The individual member owned the instruments of his trade save where they were so expensive as to necessitate corporate control." (Hilaire Belloc, *The Servile State* [1st American ed.; New York: Henry Holt and Company, 1946], pp. xiv–xv) .

142

fore, should favour ownership, and its policy should be to induce as many people as possible to become owners."[2] Paradoxically, its great protagonists, Hilaire Belloc, Gilbert Keith Chesterton, Eric Gill, and Father Vincent McNabb, O.P., were known internationally for accomplishments other than championing Distributism. Yet, it has been pointed out that

> the one truly significant thing about all four for us today is that they had in common an organic, distributist, practical sociology firmly based on the principles set out in *Rerum Novarum;* and they held it as a thing proceeding naturally and inevitably, and indeed supernaturally, from their Catholic Faith.[3]

Hilaire Belloc set forth the tenets of Distributism in 1912 in his essay *The Servile State.* After describing the distributive state, he succinctly defined it as one in which distribution of property exists to such an extent that that institution is the mark of the whole state, and free citizens are normally found to

---

[2] Husslein, *op. cit.,* p. 194.

[3] John Todd, "Distributism," *Blackfriars,* XXX (June, 1949), 280. The same author indicates that Belloc and Chesterton were appreciated as litterateurs, Gill as an artist, and Father McNabb, O.P., as a spiritual writer. (*Ibid.*). It is interesting to note that they endeavored to live what they preached, and the three laymen purchased small properties in the country, though there was no attempt at subsistence farming. Eric Gill probably carried out Distributist ideas to the greatest extent, taking as a rule "Never buy what you can make" for house and workshop. He was a Dominican Tertiary and lived semi-communally with the group at Ditchling Common. At Capel-y-ffin, Wales, 1924–1928, "no attempt was made at any organization or communal living beyond what is necessarily involved by common interests and close contiguity" (Donald Attwater (ed.), *Modern Christian Revolutionaries* [New York: The Devin-Adair Company, 1947], p. 180). This was true also of the last twelve years of his life, when he lived at High Wycombe, Buckinghamshire (*Ibid.,* p. 184). Gill attributed his introduction to Distributism and his ideas on social reform to Father McNabb, O.P. (Eric Gill, *Autobiography* [New York: The Devin-Adair Company, 1942], pp. 133, 136, 215.

be possessors of capital or land, or both.[4] And Distributism has been defined as "the theory that the political, economic and personal freedom proper to man without distinction of class or race can only be maintained when property in the means of production is widely distributed."[5] Reaction to *The Servile State* was far from dramatic, even though demand for it warranted a second edition within a year of the first publication.

Interest in Distributism was kept alive through pertinent articles in *The Eye Witness,* June, 1911–October, 1912, edited at the outset by Hilaire Belloc and subsequently by Cecil Chesterton; in the *The New Witness,* November, 1912–May, 1923, under the same editorship till 1916 and then under that of Gilbert K. Chesterton; in *G. K.'s Weekly,* 1925–1936; and in *The Weekly Review,* 1936–1947, edited by Hilary Pepler and Reginald Jebb, Belloc's son-in-law. Despite the changes in the title, the paper continued its basic policies and remained the official organ of political, social, and economic criticism and of Distributism.[6] The editors themselves took responsibility for a number of articles per issue, in addition to the editorials. Belloc's *The Servile State* and *The Restoration of Property,*[7] and Chesterton's *What's Wrong with the World* and *The Outline of Sanity,* embodying the synthesis of Distributist doctrine, appeared first as a series of articles.

---

[4] Belloc, *The Servile State,* pp. 100–101.

[5] Donald Attwater (ed.), *A Catholic Dictionary* (3rd ed.; New York: The Macmillan Company, 1958), p. 152.

[6] Maisie Ward, *Gilbert Keith Chesterton* (New York: Sheed & Ward, 1943), p. 321.

[7] The articles which formed the basis of this work appeared in *The English Review* and not in the above-mentioned periodicals (Robert Speaight, *The Life of Hilaire Belloc* [New York: Farrar, Straus & Cudahy, 1957], p. 484).

For *G. K.'s Weekly*, Eric Gill became the art critic on condition that Chesterton "accept my doctrine as the doctrine of *G. K.'s Weekly* in matters of art—just as I accept yours in other matters."[8] The "other matters" obviously were Distributism and social reform, as indicated further by Gill: "I don't intend to write for you as an outsider (have I not put almost my last quid into your blooming Company—7% or not). . . ."[9] Weekly, Belloc's contribution was on current or foreign affairs and "what would presently come of [them]."[10] Among the clergy Father Vincent McNabb, O.P., was the leading Distributist. He was a regular contributor to *G. K.'s Weekly* and was considered "a really great Distributist writer."[11] One of his provocative articles, "Fifteen Things a Distributist Can Do,"[12] however, denoted a point of divergence in Distributist doctrine which, along with the controversy over the use of machinery, would threaten the very life of Distributism. Regular contributors to the periodical, who wrote to propagandize Distributism, were not wanting—W. R. Titterton, Assistant Editor at its launching; J. Desmond Gleeson, who from first-hand knowledge has sketched the story of *G. K.'s Weekly* and the Distributist League;[13] H. S. D. Went and Maurice B. Reckitt, initial Secretary and Treasurer, respectively, of the Distributist League. Gregory MacDonald, G. C. Heseltine, Herbert Shove, Hilary Pepler, and others contributed article upon article in defense, in exposition, and in praise of Distributism. It was through *G. K.'s Weekly* "that

---

8 Quoted in Ward, *op. cit.,* p. 496.
9 Walter Shewring (ed.) , *Letters of Eric Gill* (New York: The Devin-Adair Company, 1948), pp. 190–191.
10 Ward, *op. cit.,* p. 506.
11 *Ibid.,* p. 520.
12 *G. K.'s Weekly,* XI (April 5, 1930) , 53–54.
13 Given in Maisie Ward, *Return to Chesterton* (New York: Sheed & Ward, 1952), pp. 256–277.

the ideas of Belloc, Chesterton, and some others were broad-
cast and became accessible to the public."[14] Through it the
Distributist movement has grown, and "the ideas crystallised
so as to form a definite social, economic, and political programme."[15]

The Distributist League. In 1926 Captain Went suggested
that Distributists in their own districts should unite to implement their principles.[16] *G. K.s Weekly,* by keeping all
groups in touch with one another, was to be the unifying element of the various units or clubs that might be formed. The
idea "caught fire," and the Distributist League was formally
launched at a meeting in Essex Hall, London, in September,
1926. Within three months branches had been organized in
London,[17] Birmingham, Liverpool, Manchester, Chatham,
Oxford, Glasgow, and Edinburgh.[18]

By the formation of the league the literary basis of the
Distributist movement was reinforced with a social basis.
Edward Collins, S.J., stated that now two additional aims
were added. "First, to find out how property can be distributed: secondly, to distribute it."[19] Subsequent to the found-

---

[14] Edward Collins, S.J., "Distributism," *The Irish Monthly,* LXXII
(January, 1944) , 9.

[15] *Ibid.*

[16] "W. R. Titterton claims that (Leaguers not withstanding) the
Distributist League was founded as a means of saving the paper.
He was himself he believes the originator of the idea, but Captain
Went's was chosen as the best draft of its aims and constitution"
(Ward, *Return to Chesterton,* p. 263, n.) However, the League
was formed at the time of the impending bankruptcy of the paper,
and this undoubtedly was discussed at the weekly meeting, espe-
cially since many staff members were also League members.

[17] "A London Branch was formed at the Bar of the Devereux
(a tavern near Fleet Street and the Temple) , known as the Central
Branch" (*Ibid.*) .

[18] Collins, *op. cit.,* 9.

[19] *Ibid.*

ing of the League and during its prosperity, a page in *G. K.'s Weekly* was devoted to the League, indicating activities of the branches, announcing various meetings, listing books pertinent to Distributism, and carrying the following resume of Distributist tenets.

The League offers the only practical alternative to the twin evils of Capitalism and Socialism. It is equally opposed to both; they both result in the concentration of property and power in a few hands to the enslavement of the majority.

The League stands
For the Liberty of the Individual and the Family. Against interference by busybodies, monopolies, or the State.

Personal Liberty will be restored mainly by the better Distribution of Property (i.e., ownership of land, houses, workshops, gardens, means of production, etc.).

The Better Distribution of Property will be achieved by protection and facilitating the ownership of individual enterprises in land, shops, and factories.

Thus the League fights for:
Small Shops and Shopkeepers against multiple shops and trusts. Individual Craftsmanship and Cooperation in industrial enterprise. (Every worker should own a share in the Assets and Control of the business in which he works). The Small Holder and Yeoman Farmer against monopolists of large inadequately farmed estates. And the Maximum, instead of the minimum, initiative on the part of the citizen.

At regular intervals the league arranged for public lectures and debates "to give the Distributist angle on current questions."[20] The Distributists had able spokesmen in Hilaire

[20] Ward, *Return to Chesterton*, p. 270.

Belloc,[21] G. K. Chesterton, Vincent McNabb, O.P., Eric Gill, Richard O'Sullivan, and Maurice Beckitt. Comparatively large audiences attended both lectures and debates, and with the establishment of the league the circulation of *G. K.'s Weekly* soared, yet positive reaction remained insignificant. Various other factors entered which weakened the force and appeal of Distributism.

The dichotomy which developed in the league itself over a program of action and over machinery detracted considerably from the influence it might have exercised. Chesterton, and those in agreement with him, met the pleas for action on the part of some members with insistence that, while the league hoped in time to create communities which would lead to the Distributive state, the work of the league at present "was only that of Propaganda—a wider and wider dissemination of the principles of Distributism. Their work, they said, was to talk."[22] Even more damaging was the controversy over machinery. Here, Chesterton indicated his readiness to compromise: "There may be, and . . . there are, a certain number of things that had better be always done by machinery. . . ."[23] But this was not without qualification: "I am inclined to conclude that it is quite right to use the existing machines in so far as they do create a psychology that can despise machines; but not if they create a psychology that respects them."[24] Further extenuating stipulations were manifested

[21] Despite Belloc's great part in founding Distributism itself and the league, he rarely lectured on it. His biographer attributed this to "his chronic reluctance to become a leader," or to boredom (Speaight, *op. cit.,* p. 485). Maisie Ward stated "that whereas Belloc was not unknown on the Distributist platform, he never even pretended to take any serious interest in the movement" (*Return to Chesterton,* p. 273).

[22] Ward, *Gilbert Keith Chesterton,* p. 512.

[23] *Ibid.,* p. 518.

[24] Gilbert Keith Chesterton, *The Outline of Sanity* (New York: Dodd, Mead & Company, 1927), p. 201.

in his preference "that any such necessary machine should be owned by a small local guild, on principles of profit-sharing, or rather profit-dividing; but a real profit-sharing and real profit-dividing, not to be confounded with capitalist patronage."[25] Those views were shared, to a certain extent, by Belloc and Gill, but Vincent McNabb, O.P., would have no part of them—he "regarded industrialism as such as a morally evil thing."[26] He considered its fruits as evil and, logically then, had to condemn machinery as evil. This lack of agreement among Distributists themselves, together with the fact that the central branch, which the public expected to lead the movement, acquired the reputation of beer-drinking theorists and utopians, led to a general skepticism concerning the movement.

[25] *Ibid.,* pp. 167–168.

[26] Ferdinand Valentine, O.P., *Father Vincent McNabb, O.P.* (Westminster, Maryland: The Newman Press, 1955), p. 135. He believed the machine was responsible "for the dislocation of modern life and the disintegration of the home" and therefore did without it as far as possible, sometimes walking ten, fifteen, or more miles to keep an appointment. His homespun habit was made on a domestic loom, his boots were handmade by a craftsman, and he refused to use a typewriter, and for a time, even a fountain pen (*Ibid.,* pp. 156–157). In the light of Father McNabb's regular attendance at Distributist League Meetings at the Devereux and his constant advocacy of the distribution of property, especially in the form of land and subsistence farming (cf. his twelve-point manifesto of his social philosophy, *Ibid.,* pp. 143–144), the following quotation is of particular interest: "Father Vincent wrote to Michael Sewell . . . 'July 11, 1932 . . . You say: "Kenrick has definitely said that the use of machinery is incompatible with Distributist freedom." You ask me if Kenrick's statement has my approval? You must let me withhold either approval or disapproval, because I am not a Distributist. How often have I said that I am not a *politician* nor an economist? I have, therefore, no competence to say what is or is not compatible with Distributism. The settling of that question must naturally be left to Distributists. But if you ask me, as a priest, "Is machinery with its function of mass-production, reconcilable with— WOE TO YOU THAT ARE RICH—BLESSED ARE THE POOR" the question seems to answer itself.' "

Action. While the league was severely criticized for its in-action, some defense can be tendered for proposals of action made by the founders and recommended to the government for implementation. In his *The Outline of Sanity* Chesterton set forth a "half dozen things which would help the process of Distributism":

(1) The taxation of contracts so as to discourage the sale of small property to big proprietors and encourage the break-up of big property among small proprietors. (2) Something like the Napoleonic testamentary law and the destruction of primogeniture. (3) The establishment of free law for the poor, so that small property could always be defended against great. (4) The deliberate protection of certain experiments in small property, if necessary by tariffs and even local tariffs. (5) Subsidies to foster the starting of such experiments. (6) A league of voluntary dedication.[27]

Chesterton believed that if a "patch" of peasantry were created, it would serve as a nucleus of attraction and as a magnet, and that people would withdraw from the trades and industrial life to take up subsistence farming.[28]

Belloc proposed a more definite plan in order "to reestablish the peasant, the draftsman and the small retail tradesman."[29] The main features of the plan were, first, "the handicapping of the large distributor, by differential taxation; . . . to be applied simultaneously . . . (1) against chain shops; (2) against multiple shops; (3) against large retail turnover";[30] secondly, to use the system for the artificial economic protection of the small distributor. Further, "it should be used to establish and conserve corporate credit within the guild to which . . . the

[27] p. 92.
[28] *Ibid.,* p. 143.
[29] Belloc, *Restoration of Property,* p. 72.
[30] *Ibid.*

small distributor should belong; it should even be used, . . . to subsidize the starting of the small man."[31]

Despite internal opposition, and while the central branch continued to "talk," there was some attempt at action by other branches. J. Desmond Gleeson spoke of these efforts disparagingly in his perfunctory account:

> One unfortunate feature of the League's history was the attempt to establish three or four little agricultural communities in various parts. I call it "unfortunate" because it was mainly an effort to satisfy the whim of a minority, and an "attempt to establish" because nothing was established—save only the proneness of certain Distributists to act first and think later.
>
> The matter was not important except in so far as it took up a disproportionate amount of the League's publicity, and the inevitable failure of such rash movements reflected badly on all Distributists striving to deserve a reputation for soundness of judgment. The fault of such ill-prepared movements to the land was that they were ill-advised, ill-planned and ill-equipped and manned by exactly the wrong sort of people.[32]

The Birmingham Scheme, proposed by that branch as early as 1928, and periodically revised, was the most practicable. Again, it was action through the government that was envisioned. In epitome the plan was this:

> The Birmingham Distributists would capitalize an unemployed man's present dole at the actuarial figure of £1,733, and would make up in another way a total of £2,060 to be spent in settling him on twenty-five acres for "straight" farming. The £2,060 pays not only for the freehold (to be mortgaged to the holder on a plan of thirty yearly repayments) but also sets the man up with tools and seeds. Further, it guarantees him fifteen months' preliminary

---

[31] *Ibid.*

[32] Quoted in Ward, *Return to Chesterton,* p. 274.

151

subsistence. The employed as well as the unemployed would be admitted to the ballots for these small farms, because whenever an employed man left a mill or factory for the land, his old job would fall to one of the unemployed. As for marketing the produce, the Distributists' prime desire is the creation of a peasantry feeding itself on the land and selling its surplus only. Suggestions are made for the co-operative selling of this surplus: also for the sharing of a horse and plough among five holders.[33]

Undoubtedly there would have been problems in implementing the scheme, but it did have it merits, and it was unfortunate that the government did not see fit to collaborate with the Distributists in the experiment.

In 1934, the Distributist League published a small book entitled *The Distributist Programme*. It outlined the projected distributive state and then elucidated the practical means by which it might be attained. These were enunciated under seven major headings:

1. The restraint of unjust competition.
2. The redistribution of property.
3. The creation of conditions favouring small ownerships.
4. Extended ownership of necessarily large-scale industries.
5. Measures for the conservation of distributed property.
6. The return to the land, and
7. The practice of distributist principles by the individual.[34]

As the reviewer stated, the means were "practicable enough, *if only enough people can be induced to want them.*"[35] And,

[33] "News and Notes," *The Tablet,* CLII (December 1, 1928), 707. The 1932 version of the scheme is explained in the Appendix of John McQuillan *et al., Flee to the Fields* (London: Heath Cranton Limited, 1934), pp. 217–224.
[34] Leslie Toke, Review of *The Distributist Programme,* by the Distributist League, *G. K.'s Weekly,* XIX (June 14, 1934), 234–235.
[35] *Ibid.,* 235.

indeed, that seemed to be the crux of the whole matter. Individuals who accepted the challenge of distributism wholeheartedly, and, therefore, were ready and willing to sacrifice amenities that industrialization had provided, successfully carried out subsistence farming.[36]

Pro and Con. Distributism, hearkening back to days of yore, had a distinct medieval tone. Advocates were aware of this, and one writer bluntly stated: "If a certain amount of immediate efficiency has to be sacrificed in order to satisfy the instinct for property, why, then, a certain amount of immediate efficiency has to be sacrificed."[37] It was inconceivable that large numbers would be ready for such heroism, "unless the very memory of the Industrial Revolution could be effaced from the minds of men. . . ."[38] Ruth Kenyon, tracing the line of discussion at the Anglo-Catholic summer schools of sociology held in 1928–1930, reported that

> the genuine mechanic, controller of a machine, finds as real joy in his work as ever did any manual labourer. Mechanics who were present at the School assured us of this. Housewives also arose to testify that they had no sort of preference for the old-fashioned method of duster, brush and elbow-grease over the modern Hoover.[39]

Belloc realized the radical change of attitude requisite for large scale Distributism when he wrote: "The restoration of Property must essentially be the product of a new mood, not of a new scheme. It must grow from seed planted in the breast. It is too late to reinfuse it by design. . . ."[40]

---

[36] Maisie Ward recounts some such "success stories" in *Gilbert Keith Chesterton,* pp. 521–522.

[37] Christopher Hollis, "The Case for the Distributist State," *Ave Maria,* new ser., XLVIII (December 17, 1938), 77.

[38] McEntee, *op. cit.,* p. 112.

[39] *The Catholic Faith and the Industrial Order* (London: Philip Allen, 1931), p. 95.

[40] *The Restoration of Property,* p. 11.

Though most of the Distributists were Catholics, not all Catholics accepted Distributism. Many remained totally indifferent to it, while others opposed it. Some were aware of sound basic principles in it but saw also an extremism in it. As part of the Social Catholic movement its achievements are debatable. Opposition to it on the part of the strongest element in the Social Catholic movement emphasized its weakness. In 1922 *The Christian Democrat* voiced approval:

> The Catholic Social Guild is necessarily on the side of the Distributive State. Upholding as we do the rights of private property, we are opposed to socialism because it is in conflict with that right and because it is incapable of really relieving the evils it is supposed to remedy, while, on the other hand, as advocates of liberty, we must refuse to purchase security for the labouring class by condemning labour to permanent dependence in the Servile State.[41]

After the publication of *The Outline of Sanity*, however, the Catholic Social Guild displayed a marked change of attitude, and denounced Distributism since " 'self-sufficiency' is put first and it seems to be the main object of Mr. Chesterton and distributists associated with him."[42] The Guild maintained this position, and in March, 1932, Father O'Hea, S.J., by a critical study and using *Quadragesimo Anno,* showed "the futility of the Distributists' selective interpretation of Pope Leo's encyclical."[43] Furthermore, the guild was at variance with Father McNabb's opinion on industrialism and the complete rejection of machinery. It considered Distributism "a blind alley into which went many of the young and fervent

---

[41] F. Rawlinson, "The Distributive State," *The Christian Democrat,* II (March, 1922) , 6.

[42] Henry Somerville, "Distribution and Some Distributists," *The Christian Democrat,* VII (May, 1927) , 68.

[43] Cleary, *op. cit.,* p. 119.

Catholics of the thirties. . . ."[44] In accord with the Guild's attitude was the commentary of another writer:

> The Popes seem to be more optimistic about the capitalistic system than the great "Distributists,"—G. K. Chesterton, Hilaire Belloc, . . . For the Popes confidently believe that the capitalistic system can be adjusted *according to the norms of right order,* i.e., of social justice, or the common good and they give directions for the accomplishment of this object.[45]

About 1939 the league ceased to function effectively,[46] but Distributism lived on. In 1943 *The Tablet* was defending it against the old charges that it was medieval and primarily agricultural.[47] It was also defending the view that share-holding was a form of Distributism.[48] An optimistic note on it was sounded after the war:

> In the rank and file of the Conservative Party there are men and women beginning to think of and preach on Tory platforms a mysterious thing called Distributism. . . .
>
> .   .   .   .
>
> The ultimate germ of this present ferment is the revived organization of the Distributist movement. It is literally microscopic in size, but its thought is being borrowed and expressed by all the odd movements that are now going on. With no means, with no real organization at present, with nothing but an idea, it does not reach much of the population so far, but where it does it meets generally with a good response.
>
> .   .   .   .
>
> Modern Distributists accept the presence of the industrial system but do not admit its permanence. . . .

[44] *Ibid.*
[45] Miller, *op. cit.,* pp. 201–202.
[46] Valentine, *op. cit.* p. 134.
[47] "The World Week By Week," *The Tablet,* CLXXXI (March 20, 1943), 135.
[48] *Ibid.*

The Distributists accept and state two main propositions: that ownership of property must be restored to the dispossessed proletariat; and that ownership of property means fundamentally ownership of the means of production. There is only one practical way of doing this—by co-partnership and profit-sharing.[49]

Over the years Christopher Hollis had altered his thinking to agree with this type of Distributism, as he indicated: ". . . the distributist merely evades the issue of the modern world if he contents himself with denouncing big business. We must . . . see if we can find a way of making it responsible."[50] He then suggested that plans be formulated "to spread throughout the factory confidence in policy and to give to the workers a sense of partnership in their enterprise,[51] and eventually to create "a situation where the workers are the shareholders and the shareholders are the workers."[52] His conclusion was that "we can only defeat Communism by fearlessly applying our Christian and distributist principles to our own industrial problems."[53]

But there existed the same problems and difficulties that confronted the earlier Distributists, e.g.: ". . . the real obstacle is the general paralysis of the will. More often than not there is intellectual acceptance of the idea, but that is as far as anybody gets. . . ."[54] There were also still those who believed that Distributism meant subsistence farming and small shops. Postwar periodicals carried articles reminiscent of the ideas of the 1930's, as these excerpts exemplify:

---

[49] Charles Hope, "Ferment in England," *The Catholic World,* CLXVII (August, 1948) , 412-413.

[50] "A Conservative Viewpoint," *The Christian Democrat,* new ser., I (September, 1950) , 29.

[51] *Ibid.*

[52] *Ibid.*

[53] *Ibid.*

[54] Hope, *op. cit.,* 413–414.

The starting point of distributism is the natural right of man to own property and its aim is to ensure that every family has . . . an adequate amount to subsist upon independently.[55]

. . . the number of strictly economic opportunities for real private ownership on a comparatively small scale is often overlooked. . . . Here are a few examples: all farming and its ancillary crafts; all retailing of goods; all motor transport whether for passengers or goods; all fisheries; light industries and a large percentage of building; repair shops; laundries; garages; etc., etc. If these and similar opportunities were taken, the whole social character of the country would be transformed without losing efficiency and by this transformation the task of establishing a Distributive State be made easier, for there would be an independent public opinion whose weight would be felt by the Government.[56]

Distributism persists even today, and its "official" members and guests meet annually, usually at Spode House, Hawkesyard Priory. Reporting the meeting of 1956, *The Tablet* stated that "present at the conference were representatives of the Church, the crafts, the land, local government, and the universities."[57] The post-Chesterton Distributist group was small but articulate, and in *The Weekly Review* (1938–1947), in *The Defendant* (1947–1956), and then in *The Distributist* (now defunct), it had an official organ for its written word. Hopes for the eventual success of Distributism have not been crushed. Writing in 1951, Donald Attwater stated that in his opinion "the Distributist League was before its time."[58]

---

[55] Marion Mitchell Stancioff, "Distributism," *Integrity*, III (March, 1949), 7.

[56] Reginald Jebb, "Private Property and the Distributist Thesis," *Blackfriars*, XXXI (July, 1950), 329.

[57] "Distributists at Spode House," *The Tablet*, CCVIII (October 20, 1956), 342.

[58] "The Decline of Distributism," *The Commonweal*, LIII (February 2, 1951), 422.

He did not believe Distributism had failed; he believed it had not yet had a chance to succeed.[59]

Land Movement

Associations. According to one interpretation, the Back-to-the-Land movement was a counterpart of the Distributist movement. That it grew out of Distributism can scarcely be disputed. It was particularly the Distributist group which had advocated action in the form of subsistence farming that became active in the Back-to-the-Land movement. Harold Robbins contended that "everywhere in England the Land Associations were formed when the League seemed to have reached the doldrums, and when immediate action, on a compact basis, which offered a chance of success, appeared imperative."[60]

Following the establishment of the Scottish Catholic Land Association in 1929 and the launching of its official organ, *Land for the People,* in 1930, the English Catholic Land Association was formed at London in January, 1931. In March, the Birmingham area set up the Midlands Catholic Land Association. Realizing that sectional differences had to be recognized, in June the London group became the South of England Catholic Land Association. Manchester also became interested, and in October of the same year the North of England Catholic Land Association came into existence. The Liverpool and Nottingham Catholic Land associations were founded in 1932. The six associations were united by representatives on a standing joint committee,[61] and *Land for the People* became a joint organ.

In 1934, reorganization allied the associations in The Catholic Land Federation under the chairmanship of the Right

[59] *Ibid.*

[60] "The Last of the Realists," *The Cross and the Plough,* XV (Michaelmas, 1948), 16.

[61] All data of the paragraph taken from McQuillan *et al., op. cit.,* pp. 18–19.

Reverend Monsignor Dey, D.S.O., and with Reginald Jebb as secretary. At the same time, *Land for the People* reverted to control of the Scottish association, and *The Cross and the Plough*, under the editorship of Harold Robbins, was inaugurated as the official organ of the English and Welsh Catholic Land associations. Each association had as patron the bishop, or bishops, of the respective areas; each had a clergyman as chairman and a layman as secretary. As soon as possible after organization, each association set up its own training farm. By 1934, the associations were fully developed, as indicated in Table 3.

The Right Reverend Monsignor James Dey stated that "the essential aim of the Catholic Land Associations is to establish communities of small-holding farmers with their allied secondary trades. . . ."[62] This involved a number of problems. The urbanized proletariat knew nothing of the technicalities of farming, nor did they understand that farming, especially the subsistence farming which was anticipated, constituted a way of life. It meant the individual had to undergo a program of training, coinciding with Belloc's stated principle that "you cannot make a peasant direct out of a townsman."[63] The "essential aim" implied other objectives set forth in the complete statement of aims:

> To apply to Land Settlement the principles of the Encyclicals *Rerum Novarum* and *Quadragesimo Anno,* with special reference to their insistence on the natural right of man to private property.
> To begin . . . by establishing Training Farms for as many as possible of our unemployed and over-industrialized urban people.
> To set up these trained men, with their families, in small subsistence farms to be owned and managed by the holders, and to do this, as far as possible, in communities

---

[62] "The Back to the Land Movement," *The Dublin Review,* CXCVI (April, 1935), 262.
[63] *The Restoration of Property,* p. 110.

TABLE 3
CATHOLIC LAND ASSOCIATIONS[64]

ASSOCIATION	PATRONS	CHAIRMAN	HON. SECRETARY	TRAINING FARM
Scottish	Archbishop of Glasgow	Rev. John McQuillan, D.D.	J. P. Magennis	Broadfield Farm Symington
South of England	Archbishop of Westminster Bishop of Northampton Bishop of Brentwood	Rev. Herbert Vaughan, D.D.	B. Keating	Old Brown's Farm Chartridge
Midlands	Archbishop of Birmingham Bishop of Shrewsbury Bishop of Nottingham	Rt. Rev. Msgr. J. Dey, D.S.O.	H. Robbins	West Fields Farm Market Bosworth
*North of England	Bishop of Salford	Rev. T. Fish, D.D.	D. J. Jones A.C.A.	
Nottingham	Bishop of Nottingham	Rt. Rev. Msgr. J. Bigland	H. G. Weston M.A.	Grove Farm Panton
*Liverpool	Archbishop of Liverpool	Dom Gregory Buisseret, O.S.B.	J. Gavin	Priors Wood Hall Parbold

* These two associations conducted the Priors Wood training center jointly.

[64] Reproduced from Robbins, "The Last of the Realists," 17.

of land workers and craftsmen forming fully rounded village units.

To urge constantly on the Government, and on those who have been spared the horrors of unemployment, the vital need of balancing the realm of England by restoring a land-owning Peasantry.

To educate Catholics in the need for recreating a Catholic Rural Life, and in the necessity for restoring the conception of Family Subsistence Farming to England.

To collect funds for all these objects.[65]

Insofar as the bishops had become patrons of the various Catholic Land associations, the hierarchy had accorded the movement recognition and approbation. A papal letter of approval gave further encouragement to the work undertaken by the associations; it was received by the Right Reverend Monsignor James Dey, chairman of the Catholic Land Federation, and read as follows:

Del Vaticano
1st July, 1933

Very Rev. Monsignor,

The Holy Father has heard with satisfaction of the progress already made by the five Catholic Land Associations of Great Britain, and prays this important work of restoring the sane and healthy life of the country-side may be abundantly blessed by God and result in the diminution of unemployment through the development of the agricultural resources of the country to the fullest extent possible.

As an encouragement to persevere in this good work, His Holiness most gladly imparts His Apostolic Blessing to all who are engaged in furthering this most praiseworthy enterprise.

With the assurance of my personal good wishes,

I am,

Yours very sincerely,
E. Cardinal Pacelli[66]

---

[65] Harold Robbins, "Order of Battle," *The Cross and the Plough,* XVI (Ladyday, 1949) , 5.

[66] Given in McQuillan *et al., op. cit.,* p. xi.

Such approval, however, was not forthcoming from the government. While it took no steps to deter the movement, it remained indifferent to the Catholic Land associations, and it was only after most of the experiments had ceased that any financial assistance was available through the government.

Experiments. As already indicated, training was necessary if families were to settle and farm successfully the small holdings envisioned to make up the Catholic rural communities. Apprenticeship within a Catholic farmer's household was recognized by the Catholic Land associations as the ideal and most promising method of training. The small number of Catholic farmers, and even smaller number willing to participate in such a program, prohibited the system.[67] The only way open was the establishment of training farms on which groups of men could be taught the many facets of farming. As soon as possible, each association acquired land and from the list of applicants selected the number of trainees—unmarried men because of financial limitations—that each farm could accommodate. Other personnel appointed to the farms included a warden, who was always a priest and served as chaplain to the farm community and frequently as parish priest to the surrounding rural area, a manager, bailiff, and a housekeeper.[68]

A three-year course in practical and theoretical farming was planned for the men in training. The variety of undertakings is indicated in this report on one of the farms after about two years of work:

Today there are approximately 22 cattle, 70 sheep, 50 pigs, and 300 fowl.

. . . .

The crops grown are normally used for stock and house, but some (chiefly wheat) of the produce is sold. Wheat,

---
[67] *Ibid.,* p. 83.
[68] Robbins, "The Last of the Realists," 17.

barley, oats, and maize, are grown, in addition to vetches, kale, roots, etc. There is a good kitchen garden, and fruit (in great variety) is just now plentiful and good. . . .[69]

At the annual meeting of the Midlands Catholic Land Association, Limited, in 1934 the training farm reported "the successful harvesting of thirty-three acres of corn, entirely with the scythe, spring ploughing and cultivation of forty-one acres of arable, and autumn ploughing and cultivation of twenty-seven acres. . . . Milking, buttermaking, poultry keeping and pig breeding have been features of the routine work."[70] The achievements, the associations contended, affirmatively solved the old problem "whether the townsman could be turned into a farmer."[71]

Spiritual development and training, as well as mental training, constituted part of the trainees' schedule. Each day began with Mass. The communal life on the farms required virtue and sacrifice on the part of the trainees. Archbishop Goodier, S.J., presiding at a gathering under the auspices of the South of England Catholic Land Association, commended the work of the association and then voiced appreciation of the workers' example of faith, hope, and charity, "for they had displayed great faith in the possibilities of their work, trust in God and in each other, and love of Him, and also of each other, seeing that they lived in complete harmony for many months."[72] Locally, the trainees at Old Brown's Farm were termed "the Monks of Chartridge," and a reporter felt that "the life lived on the farm is quite in keeping with this descrip-

---

[69] "Old Brown's Farm," *The Christian Democrat,* (XIV November, 1934), 166.

[70] "The Catholic Land Movement," *The Tablet,* CLXIII (February 3, 1934), 150.

[71] "The Catholic Land Movement," *The Tablet,* CLXVII (April 25, 1936), 520.

[72] "The Catholic Land Movement," *The Tablet,* CLX (December 3, 1932), 725.

tion."[73] Intellectual development was stimulated by lectures on a variety of topics. These were given by the farm staff and guest speakers. The Midlands Catholic Land Association, in 1935, announced that "the seven senior trainees have been attending a wide range of lectures arranged by the Leicestershire County Council."[74] These lectures were a means to keep abreast of agricultural science, a necessity if the farms were to succeed even on the subsistence level.[75]

Lack of funds kept the training farms of the Catholic Land associations in precarious circumstances during their entire existence. From the beginning they depended solely on the charitable donations, in goods or in currency, of the association members and other interested individuals to finance their undertakings. Government assistance had not been proffered; on the contrary, the government withdrew the unemployment insurance of the trainees on the grounds (1) that farming was not considered insurable work[76] and (2) that since settlement was the ultimate goal of the associations, the trainees were no longer potential industrial laborers.[77] Furthermore, the Midlands Catholic Land Association annual meeting of 1935 revealed that the state's only recognition of the association was " (1) a demand for income tax on a non-existent income; and (2) an intimation from the Registrar of Friendly Societies that the Association must pay Stamp Duty on it cheques."[78]

Following the unsuccessful attempts of the associations to obtain governmental assistance, "the Catholic Land Federa-

---

[73] "Old Brown's Farm," *loc. cit.*

[74] "Work on the Land," *The Tablet,* CLXV (March 16, 1935), 342.

[75] "News and Notes," *The Tablet,* CLIX (December 3, 1932), 719.

[76] "The Catholic Land Movement," *The Tablet,* CLXVII (April 25, 1936), 521.

[77] Robbins, "The Last of the Realists," 18; "The Catholic Land Movement," *The Tablet,* CLXIII (February 3, 1934), 150.

[78] "Work on the Land," *The Tablet,* CLXV (March 16, 1935), 342.

tion made sustained and reasoned representations to the principal Cabinet Ministers"[79] but met the same negative replies. Even attempts to secure aid through the Land Settlement Association[80] failed; refusal of the pound-for-pound grant was based on "the grounds that the efforts of the Federation are on behalf of a section of the population only, and also as to control and the type of farming advocated."[81] Yet, Harold Robbins contended, "in the first printed manifesto the L.S.A. proclaimed that its duty was *to experiment with all types of smallholding.*"[82]

After years of planning, discussion, and petition, in late 1937 a means was found by which trainees could receive payment through the Unemployment Assistance Board.[83] By that time, only the North of England Catholic Land Association, Ltd., now an amalgamation of the Manchester and Liverpool associations, could benefit from the concession, Old Brown's Farm and Westfields having closed in the previous year and

---

[79] Robbins, "The Last of the Realists," 19.

[80] The Land Settlement Association, a semiofficial organization with government support, was set up in August, 1934, by "the Minister of Agriculture with a preliminary grant of £50,000 provided an equal sum was forthcoming from private sources. The dominant partners in this Association were the Society of Friends and the National Council of Social Service, with Carnegie Trust co-opted later" (*Ibid.*). The Plan of the Catholic Land Associations to settle the trained men on farms of about 25 acres, to stock the farms, to erect outbuildings, and to provide the men with initial subsistence was prohibitive in cost, and may have been the reason that the Land Settlement Association refused approval, making the Catholic associations ineligible for the pound-for-pound government grant ("The Catholic Land Movement," *The Tablet*, CLXVII [April 25, 1936], 521).

[81] "The Catholic Land Federation," *The Tablet*, CLXVI (October 5, 1935), 435.

[82] Robbins, "The Last of the Realists," 20.

[83] "North of England Catholic Land Association, Ltd.," *The Tablet*, CLXX (November 20, 1937), 703.

the Nottingham Association having discontinued shortly after. The North of England Association had also cooperated with the Land Settlement Association and set up a training center in accord with its stipulations. It was, therefore, eligible for the pound-for-pound government grant, though it entailed raising £5,000. The association continued until 1942 in its activity of "training boys under the Y.M.C.A. scheme."[84]

Financial difficulties were not the sole reason for closing the training farms. In 1935, the trainees of the Midlands Catholic Land Association were nearing the completion of their three-year training course. The association was confronted with the problem of providing settlement land for independent and individual farming. Funds were a *sine qua non* if their aims were to be fully implemented. It was decided to appeal to the Archbishop of Birmingham for his approval and support of a fund drive among the Catholics and the general public. The request was submitted at a general meeting of the hierarchy, and the following response was the hierarchical decision:

15th November, 1935

Dear Mr. Robbins,

I have been waiting for the official minutes of the last meeting of the Hierarchy in order to tell you what they decided about the Catholic Land Association.

It was resolved that the Hierarchy would not at present be justified in giving any official sanction to the Catholic Land Movement, and they authorised me to say this to you. This implies that the Bishops as a body will not take any responsibility for the Movement, although of course any individual Bishop may support it in whatever way he chooses.

I feel that the comparatively small sums which the Catholic Land Settlement Associations would be able to raise would do little to remedy the defects which they are

---

84 Robbins, "The Last of the Realists," 23.

aiming at curing, and we need all the money we can raise for the building of new schools and churches in the new housing areas. This makes me very doubtful about the success of the appeal which you wish to make, and I am equally doubtful about the financial stability of your schemes for land settlement. I am sorry not to have anything more encouraging to say.

Your devoted servant in Christ,
Thomas, Archbishop of Birmingham[85]

This initiated the disintegration of the Catholic Land associations and the federation. Many members held that the associations were a form of Catholic action, and since the episcopal sanction and commission were now wanting, there was no ground for continuance.[86] *The Cross and Plough*, however, continued publication until mid-1949 when the editor announced its suspension for two reasons: his ill health, and the fact that publication was not worthwhile, because there was no indication that Church and state would change their attitude; therefore, there was no impending action.[87]

There was much criticism of the Back-to-the-Land movement as conducted by the Catholic Land associations, and it was intimated that situations other than the foregoing forced the closing of the training farms. Methods of management, unsuitability of the land, the recognition that subsistence farming was not the solution to unemployment,[88] the belief that "the scheme of subsistence farming is a theory worked out by theorists for philosophers,"[89] lack of cooperation, or individ-

---

85 *Ibid.*

86 *Ibid.*

87 Robbins, "Order of Battle," 4.

88 Second Thoughts on Back to the Land," *The Tablet,* CLXVI (December 28, 1935) , 841–842. The article is based on a small book, *The Agricultural Dilemma,* by Lord Astor and Mr. B. Seebohm Rowntree.

89 Dom Gregory Buisseret, O.S.B., "The Catholic Land Associations," *The Tablet,* CLXX (August 14, 1937) , 22.

ualism, among the Associations, and the indifference of the Catholic body as a whole contributed to the dissolution of the Catholic Land Federation, the associations, and their undertakings.

Another experiment in land resettlement was conducted under Catholic auspices. The Marydown Farming Association operated in the south of England. In common with the Catholic Land Federation was its philosophy of settlement; in other areas its policies differed. Financial stability was secured by the issue of "interest-bearing shares for purchase by the public on business lines, and a certain capital was subscribed. On the land bought and equipped by this capital a few families were settled, and have continued up to the present time [1936] working their holdings."[90] Training was not part of the scheme, and therefore the holders selected were men who had had experience in farming. The Marydown settlement covered approximately 200 acres. Other schemes for family settlement were proposed and worked out in theory, but, with no government assistance available, they did not materialize. One scheme on the basis of a cooperative society had a realistic approach, but to raise the £100,000 initial fund required was an impossibility in the financially straitened years of the 1930's.[91]

In addition to the land settlement schemes there were experiments in training farm laborers—chiefly the youth, fourteen to eighteen years of age. Underlying the scheme was the aim to take the boys off the street and save them from delinquency, and to assist in stemming the "leakage" from the Church. Although several independent centers were established, in the main they were conducted along the same lines,

---

[90] "The Catholic Land Movement," *The Tablet,* CLXVII (April 25, 1936), 520.

[91] "News and Notes," *The Tablet,* CLIX (December 3, 1932), 719. The item gives an outline of the general plan.

following the Y.M.C.A., which had done the pioneer work in this field. A hostel, or home, was secured where the boys underwent three months of "disciplining and reconditioning,"[92] and at the same time helped in the chores requisite for the upkeep of the hostel and its farm. After this period the boys were placed with Catholic farmers (or with farmers where facilities for practicing their faith were guaranteed), who lodged them, taught them farming, and paid them a sum which, with the board and training, equated the accepted salary of a farm laborer. The superintendent of the hostel kept in touch with the boys for eighteen months, and "at the end of that time they are considered to have got a start in life, and to be worth a living wage—at all events they are set up bodily and mentally and are fit for nearly any job."[93] It was estimated that £20 was necessary to keep a boy during his stay at the hostel. The whole system was known as the National Scheme for Training Boys for Farm Employment and "received . . . support and encouragement from the Ministry of Labour, who have undertaken to grant a sum of £8 for each boy who is fully trained and placed with a farmer without displacing existing labour and in accordance with the Agricultural Wages Board Act."[94] Approval of the scheme was also accorded by Cardinal Bourne, the Bishop of Hexham and Newcastle, and the Bishop of Lamus. They endorsed a press appeal for the additional funds needed and for the formation of national and diocesan committees.[95] Until the outbreak of World War II hundreds of boys were trained under the system, and again proved that the townsman could become an efficient farmer.

[92] Mrs. R. T. Bower, "Back to the Land for Catholic Boys," *The Christian Democrat,* XIV (October, 1934), 154.

[93] Buisseret, *op. cit.,* 223.

[94] "Farm Training: The National Scheme," *The Tablet,* CLXIV (November 10, 1934), 604.

[95] "Land, Land!" *The Tablet,* CLXIII (June 2, 1934), 687.

The effort of Catholics in the Back-to-the-Land movement had a bearing on the Social Catholic movement. Indirectly, it helped to make the public aware of the pitfalls in industrial capitalism and, in many instances, developed again a sense of true values. The unrealistic, utopian experiments, however, often drew censure upon the Church. Until December, 1935, *The Tablet* wholeheartedly supported and advocated the Back-to-the-Land movement, but it lost faith in the Movement as a cure-all. *The Christian Democrat*, too, generally held aloof from the land settlement schemes. A correspondent queried, "Why is it that you will not give the land its correct place in your thought and studies?"[96] He continued: "You now engage a reviewer who attempts to ridicule the perfectly honest intellectual convictions of the ever growing body of clergy and laity who challenge the use of machinery."[97] Replied the editor: "We do not find anything in Catholic teaching or in the nature of the industry to justify the view that machinery is of the devil."[98] This statement is certainly in keeping with the counsel of Pope John XXIII that

> agriculture should receive special help, in order to permit it to use the newly-devised methods of production, types of farm management and cultivation that the economic system as a whole allows or requires. As far as possible, all these innovations should be introduced in agriculture as much as in the industrial and service sectors.[99]

The Sword of the Spirit

Early Aims and Activities. By the summer of 1940 England had not yet experienced the full, stark realities of World War II. Discerning individuals, however, were aware of

[96] "Correspondence," *The Christian Democrat*, XIII (December, 1933), 176.
[97] *Ibid.*
[98] *Ibid.*
[99] *Mater et Magistra*, p. 37.

divisive factors at work, and perceived an undercurrent of secularism and paganism that had a threefold fountainhead of bitter waters in "Nazism, with its glorification of a particular race, Communism, with its glorification of a particular class, and Fascism, with its glorification of the State. . . ."[100] To "wake up Catholics in particular, but all Christians in the country,"[101] and to effect the unity demanded for an intense effort to bring about a "true, just and lasting peace,"[102] Cardinal Hinsley founded the movement which he designated the Sword of the Spirit. Through the movement the Cardinal hoped to carry out the commission given him when he took up his duties at Westminster.[103] Christopher Dawson stated that "the essential purpose of the Movement is . . . the organization and co-ordination of our spiritual forces against the evil forces, that are attempting to conquer the world."[104] Immediately, then, the movement assumed an international scope, though activities were, by necessity, at first confined to national boundaries.

The inaugural meeting of the Sword of the Spirit was held on August 1, 1940; Cardinal Hinsley presided and Archbishop Godfrey, Apostolic Delegate, was present. Christopher Dawson, "the ablest defence of Christian values among English writers,"[105] was appointed lay leader by the Cardinal, and he later became vice-president of the society. From the begin-

---

[100] Douglas Woodruff, "The First Ten Years," *The Sword*, XI (September, 1950), 34.

[101] *Ibid.*

[102] "The Sword of the Spirit," *The Tablet*, CLXXVI (August 10, 1940), 116.

[103] The parting words of Pope Pius XI to Cardinal Hinsley were: "Take to the Catholics of England this message . . .: Before all, unity; after all, unity; everywhere unity; in all places unity; at all costs unity" (*Ibid.*).

[104] "Propaganda," *The Tablet*, CLXXVI (October 5, 1940), 266.

[105] John C. Heenan, *Cardinal Hinsley* (London: Burns, Oates & Washbourne Ltd., 1944), p. 183.

ning, the roster of persons interested and active in the movement was impressive, for it quickly captured the public imagination. The leaders were an outstanding group

> combining most of the diverse elements in Catholic life. Bishop Myers often represented the Cardinal and Father John Murray, S.J., was theological adviser. Other priests included Fr. Leo O'Hea from C.S.G., Fr. Andrew Beck, Fr. Herbert Keldany and myself [Fr. Agnellus Andrew, O.F.M.]. But the movement itself was primarily a lay movement, and its genius attracted and held a powerful and varied group. Christopher Dawson's mind gave the original bias to all our work. Paul Kelly, Richard O'Sullivan, Douglas Woodruff were chairmen in turn. Barabara Ward, A. C. F. Beales and Dr. Laetitia Fairfield were secretaries; and round the table at executive meetings you might see Bernard Sullivan, the Trade Union Leader; Arnold Lunn, the alpinist, author and apologist; Gerard Young from his steel works in Sheffield; Professor Bodkin from the Institute of Fine Arts in Birmingham; Mr. Doyle from Liverpool; together with Lady Winifred Elwes, Fr. Eugene Langdale, Fr. Gervase Mathew, O.P., Mr. R. P. Roche and Mr. Philip Coverdale, to mention only a few of that grand company.[106]

A statement, drawn up by the executive committee, set forth the fundamental aim of the movement and the methods by which it hoped to accomplish the goal:

> Fundamental Aim:—
>
> The restoration in Europe of a Christian basis for both public and private life by a return to the principles of international order and Christian freedom; for these principles are rooted in the Law of Nature which is common to all mankind and recognises no superiority of race or colour.
>
> To This End: 1. We will make clear that these nat
> The Issue. ural principles and this Christian
> conception of life are at stake in the

---

[106] Agnellus Andrew, O.F.M., "A New Campaign," *The Sword*, XI (September, 1950), 30.

	present war: since the Nazi way of life denies all the natural rights that Christianity upholds—the rights of God, of man, of the family, of minorities, of dependent peoples.
The War.	2. We will therefore fight for our cause till victory.
The Settlement.	3. After victory, the reconstruction of Europe must be based upon these same natural and Christian principles.
The Movement.	4. It is our aim to unite the citizens of this country in support of the principles at stake in this war and in the future peace.[107]

The committee issued also an official statement of principles and policy which provided the framework within which all activities were to proceed, and within which all speakers and lecturers were to act:

(1) The Movement stands for the principles of Christianity and the Natural Law;

(2) Our opposition to Nazism and other Totalitarianisms is the result of their DENIAL of these principles;

(3) Our support of the national cause rests upon this positive basis;

(4) The Post-War Settlement must be based on these principles;

(5) The Movement—for victory as a means to this Settlement—is a national movement addressed, through its Catholic sponsors, to every citizen in the Kingdom.[108]

In addition, at every function or activity conducted under the auspices of the Sword of the Spirit the purpose of the movement had to be explained. No topic or occasion was to override the importance of the stated aims.

---

[107] "The Sword of the Spirit," *The Tablet*, CLXXVL (August 10, 1940), 117.

[108] "Statement of Policy for the Guidance of Lecturers and Speakers," *The Sword of the Spirit*, Bulletin No. 2 (August 23, 1940) , n.p.

At the first week-end school held on October 5–6, 1940, Cardinal Hinsley elaborated on the two-point program determined for the Sword of the Spirit: (1) the sanctity of the family, and the value of child life; (2) the unity of international society. Indicating the basic significance of these areas, the Cardinal, anticipating wholehearted support, declared, "With all our might and main we members of the Society of The Sword of the Spirit are determined to uphold the sanctity of the family on which the soundness of each nation depends, and the Brotherhood of men in Christ on which international peace through order and justice and charity rests."[109]

Widespread interest in the movement was spontaneous. A bulletin, *The Sword of the Spirit*, issued biweekly, informed readers of plans, activities, and growth of the movement. People were eager for directions for participation in the movement, and the second issue of the bulletin carried a list of what could be done by every interested individual. Prayer for the intentions of the movement was given priority. Attention was called to the various ways in which the movement could be propagated, and circulation of the bulletin increased. Other suggestions were:

(5) Watch the national Press and the local Press and the B.B.C., and *send at once* to Headquarters full particulars of any recorded activity that is *in any way* the kind of thing that the Movement is out to encourage. Send us the cutting. *At the same time,* write to the paper or the B.B.C. yourself in warm support of the particular matter.

(6) Watch similarly for points that need correction or refutation; . . . If you can deal with these by means of an immediate letter, do so. If you cannot, for lack of information, send the cutting to Headquarters for the necessary action.

(7) Ask your parish priest whether there is as yet any

109 "The Sword of the Spirit," *The Tablet,* CLXXVI (October 12, 1940), 298.

174

activity on behalf of the Movement in your parish. If
there is, the leaders will need your help in many ways;
e.g. distribution of pamphlets, stewardship at meetings, etc. . . . If there is no local group yet active,
start one and write to Headquarters on how to proceed.

(8) Make it your business to get and distribute as many
copies as you can of each pamphlet or leaflet issued. . . .

(9) Master the contents of these pamphlets. The totali-
tarians have *their* gospel, and they know it from A to
Z. The principles of Christianity and of the Natural
Law are things we *must* understand; and we must be
able to apply them to present day questions. For this
purpose, join your nearest Catholic Social Guild
Group.[110]

These recommendations corresponded to the three headings
under which all activities of the movement were grouped:
prayer, study, action. The Sword of the Spirit was not intended as a departmental activity; it was to be lived, and
therefore entered into the individual's everyday life.[111]

Not only were the prayers of members and associate members solicited. Everyone interested was urged to pray for its
success. Intensification of the individual's spiritual life and a
clearer understanding of his religion were considered basic
to the progress and achievements of the movement. Consequently, supplementary spiritual activities were afforded in
the noonday sermons and benediction in various city churches,
in opportunities for retreats and days of recollection, in ob-
servance of a Sword of the Spirit Sunday and the celebration
of the feast of Christ the King, and in the supplied reading
materials.

---

[110] "What You Can Begin to Do at Once," *The Sword of the
Spirit,* Bulletin No. 2 (August 23, 1940), n.p.

[111] "The Spiritual Foundation," *The Sword of the Spirit,* Bulletin
No. 7 (November 2, 1940), 2–3.

Religious orders and communities participated in the movement by offering their prayers and good works on certain days of the month, and having a Mass offered on the respective days for the intentions of the society. At first these were listed in the bulletin so that on "unclaimed" days spiritual fortification might be contributed by others. In addition to the Prayer League or Rota, convents aided the movement by engaging speakers to inform the religious of the aims, immediate and long-range, of the Sword of the Spirit. Occasionally the religious offered to lecture on the movement. At other times "Convents have opened their premises for various gatherings, youth rallies, special lectures or sermons. In some cases activities of the S.O.S. have been centered round a Convent School or College. Similarly Convents have given people Study Groups, days of recollection and other facilities for prayer and study."[112]

Study of the day's problems and conditions, and of the Christian principles underlying national and international affairs, was highly encouraged. It was the means by which Christians could learn their responsibilities and the contribution they could make to Christian reconstruction. Those desiring more formal study were advised to join the C.S.G. study clubs or to form their own. Study plans to guide discussion groups were provided. In the first year of the movement there was prepared a whole series on the "basic Christian teaching on the Human Person, the Family, Society, etc., in the light of Christian doctrine and Natural Law. Another has been published on Catholicism and International Order."[113] Also available to study clubs, and for individual study, were the C.S.G. publications and those of The Sword

---

[112] A. C. F. Beales, "The Hon. Secretary's Report, 1941–42," *The Sword of the Spirit,* Bulletin No. 51 (October 29, 1942), 5.

[113] "Report," *The Sword of the Spirit,* Bulletin No. 27 (August 21, 1941), 4.

of the Spirit in the form of leaflets, pamphlets, and Sword of the Spirit papers.[114]

But study was not to be an end in itself. If action did not ensue, if the social teachings of the Church were not applied to society, if the study group did not aim at such application, the work might well end in frustration. Yet the Sword of the Spirit was in no way to be construed as a political party, and no action was to be undertaken in its name. Rather, individuals and groups were to act in the spirit of personal conviction and understanding of the Christian principles necessary for social justice and true, lasting peace. Action was to have as its basis the ten points set forth in a letter published in *The Times* on December 21, 1940, with Cardinal Hinsley, the archbishops of Canterbury and York, and the president of the Free Church Federal Council as signatories. The letter reproduced "the five peace points of Pius XII for the ordering of international relations, and appended to them five 'standards by which economic situations and proposals may be tested.' "[115] In his Christmas Message, 1939, Pope Pius XII laid down requisites for a just international peace:

---

[114] During its first year of operation the Sword of the Spirit published the following leaflets: *The Pope and the War, Christianity and International Order, Catholics Under the Swastika, Nazism and the Family, The Mission of England, For the Forces, The Women's Services, Nazis or Neighbours, Master Race or Equal Peoples, Man or Beast, The War and the Coloured Races (Ibid., 3).* Second year publications were: Leaflets—*Hitler's War on Russia, Nazism Versus Christianity, Atlantic Charter, The World We Should Like to Create, Call to Youth, Well Done, Malta!, The Struggle for the Church in Germany, A Nation United.* Pamphlets—Christopher Dawson, *The Sword of the Spirit;* Barbara Ward, *The Defence of the West;* Robert Speaight, *The Voice of the Vatican;* M. R. Adamson, *The Mask and the Face;* Michael Fogarty, *Vocation in Work; The Sword of the Spirit; What It Is and What It Does.* Sword of the Spirit Papers— *Questionnaire on the Ten Points,* Nos. 1–10; *A Family Wage—The Case of Family Allowances,* No. 11 (Beales, ". . . Report, 1941–42," 5).

[115] "Catholics and the Future of Europe," *The Tablet* CLXXVI (December 28, 1940), 504.

1. . . . assurance from all nations, great or small, powerful or weak, of their right to life and independence. The will of one nation to live must never mean the sentence of death passed upon another. When this equality of rights has been destroyed, attacked or threatened, order demands that reparation shall be made, and the measure and extent of that reparation is determined not by the sword nor by the arbitrary decision of self-interest, but by the rules of justice and reciprocal equity.

2. The order thus established (i.e. by the recognition of the right of every nation to independence), if it is to continue undisturbed and ensure true peace, requires that the nations be delivered from the slavery imposed upon them by the race of armaments, and from the danger that material force, instead of serving to protect the right, may become an overbearing and tyrannical master. Any peaceful settlement which fails to give fundamental importance to a mutually agreed organic and progressive disarmament, spiritual as well as material, or which neglects to ensure the effective and loyal implementing of such an agreement, will sooner or later show itself to be lacking in coherence and vitality.

3. . . . some juridical institution which shall guarantee the loyal and faithful fulfilment of conditions agreed upon and which shall in case of recognised need revise and correct them.

4. If a better European settlement is to be reached there is one point in particular which should receive special attention: it is the real needs and the just demands of nations and populations, and of racial minorities. It may be that, in consequence of existing treaties incompatible with them, these demands are unable to establish a strictly legal right. Even so, they deserve to be examined in a friendly spirit with a view to meeting them by peaceful methods and even, where it appears necessary, by means of an equitable and covenanted revision of the treaties themselves. If the balance between nations is thus adjusted and the foundation of mutual confidence thus laid many incentives to violent action will be removed.

5. Even the best and most detailed regulations will be powerless and foredoomed to failure unless the peoples and those who govern them submit willingly to the influence of that spirit which alone can give life, authority and binding force to the dead letter of international agreement. They must develop that sense of deep and keen responsibility which measures and weighs human statutes according to the sacred and inviolable standards of the law of God; they must cultivate that hunger and thirst after justice which is proclaimed as a beatitude in the Sermon on the Mount and which supposes as their natural foundation the moral virtue of justice; they must be guided by that universal love which is the complement and most general expression of the Christian ideal and which therefore may serve as a common ground also for those who have not the blessings of sharing the same faith with us.[116]

The appended five points, "derived from the conclusions of a Church of England Congress held at Oxford shortly prior to the war,"[117] were:

(1) That extreme inequality in wealth and possessions should be abolished.

(2) Every child, regardless of race or class, should have equal opportunities of education suitable for the development of his peculiar capacities.

(3) The family as a social unit must be safeguarded.

(4) The sense of the divine vocation must be restored to man's daily work.

(5) The resources of the earth should be used as God's gifts to the whole human race, and used with due consideration for the needs of the present and future generation.[118]

---

[116] Vincent A. Yzermans (ed.), *The Major Addresses of Pope Pius XII* (St. Paul: The North Central Publishing Company, 1961), Vol. II: *Christian Messages,* pp. 29–31.

[117] John Murray, S.J., "The Story of Cooperation," *The Sword,* XI (September, 1950), 41.

[118] "Catholics and the Future of Europe," *loc. cit.*

Study groups, branches, and local groups had access to reports on the practical implications of the ten points, but they were to work out, in terms of their own communities, the most profitable activities. Voluntary services connected with the war were considered excellent channels for disseminating knowledge of, and for putting into practice, Christian principles. Active participation in civic life was consistently encouraged as a means of influencing social and economic legislation. In September, 1941, it was suggested by Bernard Sullivan that expert committees be established to study, and prepare reports on questions involved in postwar problems. Committees were organized to investigate the following problems:

Hospitals.—Problem, Public and Voluntary. Medical services and Insurance to cover wives and dependents. Assistance Boards to cover sick cases.

Houses.—Planning and Siting Houses. Siting of industries. Transport and green belt. Churches and Schools problem. Parishes may have to be replanned in view of shifting population.

Social Welfare.—Abolition of Poor Law Taint. Distribution of functions over other services. *Outdoor Relief*: Such cases to have assistance Boards as O.A.P. and Unemployed. *Institutions*: Provision of smaller homes for single persons or old couples to end Institutions. Casual and Voluntary Homes. Set up Shelters and Soup Kitchens.

Public Utilities.—Gas; Electricity; Water; Transport.

Industrial Democracy.—Joint Councils of Industry. Trade Union Membership. Licensing of new firms. Post School Training.

Banking.—Control of Finance. Finance and Industry. Finance and Purchasing Power.

Insurance.—Linking up of insurance. Fire, Life, Health, Unemployment.

Local Authorities.—Their future and functions. Rural districts. Urban Districts, Boroughs. County Boroughs. County Councils.[119]

[119] "Expert Sub-Committees," *The Sword of the Spirit*, Bulletin No. 38 (January 22, 1942), 8.

Intensive studies of the prevailing conditions and needs were conducted and, on the basis of the research, plans and schemes were formulated to ameliorate and/or revolutionize situations. Memoranda were submitted to headquarters for use in discussion groups and study clubs. Articles and recommendations popularized the ideas through Sword publications. Probably the most revolutionary plan was that drawn up, on lines recommended by Pope Pius XI in *Quadragesimo Anno,* for the establishment of industrial democracy, which the committee defined as "a system in which each industry is recognised as being a corporate whole consisting of all those engaged in it."[120] In the preamble of the plan it was stated: "The reconstruction of Industry requires its ordered government in accordance with Christian principles. The government of Industry in the future needs to be related to the fundamental object of human life,"[121] which was basic to the plan for a new social and industrial order. Benjamin Masse perceived the revolutionary character of the system:

> That is a simple, forthright and very revolutionary statement. . . . It implies a definite break with nineteenth-century Capitalism which "has permeated our life with false values and material standards, forgetting that man does not live by bread alone." It implies an even more definite break with Socialism and Communism, systems which grew out of the irreligious, bourgeois mentality of the last century and which pretended to remove the evils of Capitalism by widening devotion to the Golden Calf.[122]

The quiet, unostentatious work of the expert committees produced worthwhile, thought-provoking studies.

As the movement progressed, its immediate aims and undertakings became more clear-cut though the founding purpose

---

120 "Industrial Democracy," Sword Paper No. 12, *The Sword of the Spirit,* Bulletin No. 53 (January 7, 1943), 5.

121 *Ibid.*

122 "Sword of Spirit Drawn for Christian Order," *America,* LXVIII (March 20, 1943) , 649.

to combat totalitarianism remained intact. In an address given in October, 1942, the Cardinal "laid down the main lines of work for the year . . . Education and Social Security."[123] To carry out the mandate, "it was recommended that there should be a campaign of prayer, and study, and action, within the framework of the Joint Pastoral of June 21st last, in three fields:— (1) Education. (2) Industry and the Social Services. (3) Good reading."[124] The campaign was to be conducted "by harnessing every Sword activity, especially Discussion Groups, Public Meetings, Study Schemes, Reading Lists, collaboration in the work of every Catholic society that concerns itself with the problem[s]."[125] Articles on all phases of the social and economic problems and of the education question were published, and the government white paper on education was fully discussed. The Sword also "took an active part in promoting parochial Catholic Parents and Electors' Associations on the Education question."[126]

[123] Barbara Ward and A. C. F. Beales, "Report of the Hon. Secretaries, 1942–43," *The Sword of the Spirit,* Bulletin No. 62 (October 7, 1943), 5.

[124] A. C. F. Beales, "Outline Plan of Work for the Year 1943," *The Sword of the Spirit,* Bulletin No. 52 (December 3, 1942), 5. Points of the joint pastoral to be considered were: " (2) The payment of this [living] wage should be the first charge on every industry. (3) The Chief factors that should determine the amount of a man's wage are (*a*) an agreed standard of work, (*b*) the capacity of the industry to pay, (*c*) an agreed minimum average family, e.g., father, mother, and three or four children. (4) When an employer cannot pay this minimum living wage, the difference should be made up. This could be done either by industry pooling a percentage of all wages paid and sharing the proceeds according to needs; or, in default of this, by the State. . . . (9) Religious education, to meet the wishes of the parents, should be available to all school children, and on such conditions that the general education of the child should not suffer in any way from its parents' insistence on religious education" (Quoted from Gordon, *op. cit.,* pp. 205–206).

[125] Beales, "Outline Plan . . .," *loc. cit.*

[126] Ward and Beales, *loc. cit.*

character of the Movement could be safeguarded only if Associate Membership carried with it no voting power and if each Ordinary had control of the Movement in his Diocese."[141]

Under the new terms non-Catholics were free to withdraw from membership, with refunded dues, if they so wished. Meanwhile, negotiations continued for a sound basis for cooperation. At the Stoll meetings it was precisely stated that "the cooperation does not . . . extend to doctrine and belief,"[142] so that compromising the faith was not involved. "We cannot compromise on any article of faith proposed to our belief by the unerring voice of the one Church of Jesus Christ . . ."[143] was the resolute stand of the Sword of the Spirit. Nevertheless, Cardinal Hinsley was convinced that cooperation was possible, and pointed out areas in which it might be carried on profitably:

> Before everything else, we desire to eliminate all bitterness in religious controversy and to cultivate a spirit of friendly intercourse among those who bear the name of Christ. Next, we want to unite on practical measures to defend the inheritance of Christian principles on which our civilization has been built. . . . Surely there are such practical measures which we can calmly discuss and adopt. There is, for example, the question of family allowances. . . . Many other social problems may approach solution by mutual understanding of their practical import.[144]

The problem of the moral justification of cooperation was fully discussed by L. L. McReavy, Professor of Canon Law at Ushaw. His conclusion was that collaboration was lawful on the basis of the "admitted distinction between the objective

---

[141] *Ibid.*

[142] "The Stoll Meetings," *op. cit.,* 193.

[143] "Presidential Address," *The Sword of the Spirit,* Bulletin No. 27 (August 21, 1941) , 2.

[144] *Ibid.,* 1.

law of right and wrong and the subjective duty of the individual to follow his conscience."[145] To corroborate Cardinal Hinsley's stand on Christian cooperation there were attestations of the popes before, during, and since his time:

Pope Leo XIII, September 18, 1895:

. . . that the usefulness of these gatherings may not be limited to Catholics, they *can be held on the understanding* that all may enter as listeners, including those who are *separated from the Catholic Church.* . . .

---

[145] "Collaboration with Non-Catholics," *The Tablet*, CLXXIX (May 23, 1942), 257. McReavy's explanation was: "Objectively, our doctrine of the oneness of the Faith rules out such collaboration, not only because it can be misinterpreted as approval of error, but also because its effect is to secure to non-Catholic bodies an authority in religious propaganda which is the exclusive right of the one true Church of Christ. But in human relations, the objective law is not the whole law. Whatever God has actually ordained, it must always remain the subjective duty of the human individual to follow the dictate of his certain conscience, because, in the final issue, that is his only key to the will of God. . . .

"It is on this basis of respect for the law of conscience that . . . we erect the structure of our everyday relations with non-Catholics. . . . It is for this reason that we admit to membership, not of the Body but at least of the Soul of the Church, all believers in Christ who genuinely follow Him according to their lights; and that we regret any decrease in their numbers and vigour other than that which results from conversion to the Catholic Church. We would suggest, therefore, that for the same reason and on the same basis we may rightly welcome the co-operation of our non-Catholic brethren in the common defence of our Christian freedom. Provided always that in fighting the common battle for religious education in the schools, and freedom of religious propaganda and ministration, we continue to stress our basic doctrine of the unity of Faith and the right of the Catholic Church alone to speak for Christ, our attitude cannot logically be interpreted as approval of error. We simply admit that our non-Catholic comrades, in fighting for the same freedoms, are only doing their imperative moral duty. And so, while we continue to strive to win them to objective truth, and to insist on its objective evidence, we welcome their co-operation as men of good will whose efforts to serve God are not without benefit to our own." (p. 257).

Pope Pius X, September 24, 1912:

We affirm, nevertheless, that *Catholics have the right, with all due* safeguards, to unite with non-Catholics for the common good, in bettering the state of labour, in obtaining juster wages and fairer working conditions, and for any good and useful project.

Pope Pius XI, March 19, 1937:

. . . it is *Our fond hope* that, besides the host which glories in the name of Christ, all those . . . who still believe in God and pay him homage may take a decisive part.

Pope Pius XII, November 1, 1939:

. . . We are *impelled by charity to invite* here the co-operation of those, whom Mother Church mourns as separated from her Communion.

Pope Pius XII, September 1, 1944:

Accordingly, to all our sons and daughters throughout the vast world, and also to those who, while not belonging to the Church, feel themselves united with us in this hour of perhaps irrevocable decision, we address an urgent appeal to weigh the extraordinary gravity of the moment and to consider that, above and beyond all such co-operation with other diverse ideological tendencies and social forces that may perhaps be suggested by purely contingent motives, fidelity to the heritage of Christian civilization and its strenuous defence against atheist and anti-Christ tendencies, is the keystone which can never be sacrificed for any transitory advantage or for any shifting combination.

The invitation which, we trust, will find a sympathetic welcome from millions of souls throughout the world, looks chiefly to achieve a loyal and effective collaboration in all those fields in which the very idea of Christianity demands the creation of a more exact juridical order. This is especially true of that group of formidable problems which refer to the setting up of an economic and social order more in keeping with the eternal law of God and with the dignity of man.[146]

Further approval was given to cooperation by the Holy See in 1945, when, under its auspices, the "new international association, *Unitas,* for the promotion of union among all Christians,"[147] was founded. In the present day, Pope John XXIII has added approbation, though a word of warning is included:

In their socio-economic activities Catholics often find themselves in close contact with others who do not share their view of life. In these circumstances, those who bear the name of Catholics should be very careful to be consistent and to avoid compromises that will involve a watering down of religion or morality. At the same time, however, let them show themselves animated by a spirit of understanding and disinterestedness, ready to co-operate loyally in achieving objectives that of their nature are good or at least reducible to good.[148]

By the spring of 1942, negotiations on cooperation had borne fruit, and in June, on the authority of the joint standing committee, composed of representatives of Religion and Life[149] and The Sword of the Spirit, the following statement was issued:

146 The foregoing are quoted from "The Popes and Christian Co-operation," *The Sword of the Spirit,* Bulletin No. 83 (July, 1945), 5.

147 "The Official Vatican Documents on Christian Co-operation," *The Sword,* No. 90 (February, 1949), 13.

148 *Mater et Magistra,* p. 63.

149 The Commission of the Churches for International Friendship and Social Responsibility, composed of Anglican and Free church representatives, established the organization known as Religion and Life "to do, within the Church of England, the Church of Scotland and the Free Churches, what The Sword of the Spirit does inside the Roman Catholic Church, so that individuals or groups, moved by public meetings or otherwise, can be linked up." ("The Joint Statement on Christian Co-operation," *The Tablet,* CLXXIX [May 30, 1942], 270).

(1) We agree that a compelling obligation rests upon all Christian people in this country to maintain the Christian tradition and to act together to the utmost possible extent to secure the effective influence of Christian teaching and witness in the handling of social, economic and civic problems, now and in the critical post-war period.

. . . .

(2) We agree that there is a large area of common ground on which, without raising ultimate questions of Church order and doctrine which divide us, full co-operation is possible and is already taking place.

. . . .

(3) We agree that organized Christianity, to fulfil its proper function, must everywhere be secured in certain essential freedoms. Full freedom must mean freedom to worship according to conscience, freedom to preach, teach, educate and persuade (all in the spirit of Christian charity), and freedom to bring up children in the faith of their parents. . . .

. . . .

(4) Our purpose is to unite informed and convinced Christians all over the country in common action on broad lines of social and international policy.

. . . .

(5) The striking thing about the Sword of the Spirit and similar movements is the spontaneity of support which they have received, and the great local enthusiasm which has accompanied public meetings arranged on this wide co-operative basis. Local spontaneity and freedom are of the highest value, and must not be overloaded by central organization. But, in our judgment, there must be a Joint Committee to give advice, direction and encouragement to all who seek it, and to extend this joint movement to parts of the country it has not yet reached.

Linked by this Committee, the two Movements will work through parallel action in the religious, and joint action in the social and international field.[150]

[150] "Religion and Life," *The Sword of the Spirit,* Bulletin No. 46 (June 4, 1942), 3.

In accord with the statement, cooperation was henceforth carried on in the manner indicated, and joint weeks and meetings were conducted throughout England. Generally, local Christian councils were established to plan and direct the functions. The earliest of these was founded at Norwich in 1940, and by the end of 1943 there were fifty councils actively engaged in promoting cooperation. For joint weeks, two dominant patterns were followed:

1. The *HITCHIN* Model . . . simultaneous denominational religious meetings each night of the week, successively on one of the Ten Points. One or more Joint Meetings, during the week, on the Ten Points Programme, with the civic authorities on the platform and a front rank speaker from each of the three main Christian streams. Usually, a Youth Rally on the Saturday to close.

2. *NOTTINGHAM* Model is completely interdenominational in its organization and exclusively civic in its joint action; i.e., Council and all Committees function on a rotation system which ignores denominational representation since on the civic plane such representation is irrelevant.[151]

Basic to the success of the councils were the study groups, which were either denominational or interdenominational. Information, knowledge, and "know-how" provided by the study groups enabled the councils to undertake various campaigns, e.g., by means of the press, on the education question and on juvenile delinquency. Local problems were also solved through the Christian councils acting as pressure groups on the parties concerned. Instances of such achievement were:

Saving the churches from being closed on Sunday morning on account of Home Guard parades. Protecting the young by making representations to local factories against the practice of employing boys and girls of 14–16 in the

---

[151] A. C. F. Beales, "Local Christian Councils," *The Sword of the Spirit,* Bulletin No. 66 (February 3, 1944) , 6.

making and testing of contraceptives. Averting a dissipa-
tion into war savings collections of the time that should
be spent in the local schools on Religious instruction. . . .
Advising local authority on suitable premises for a Youth
Organization. Securing facilities in the local factories
for religious worship during work on Sunday morning:
i.e., right of entry for denominational clergy into the
factories on Sundays. Advising Public Library on book
selection in the sphere of religion and ethics. Approaching
Board of Education in criticism of the T.U.C. Memorandum against Denominational teaching in schools.[152]

Collaboration reached its high-water mark in the second
half of 1942 and in the first half of 1943; then, ebb tide set
in, and the joint Christian meetings have been considered

a feature of the war years and, broadly speaking, did not
survive the war, and they might be classed among what
Mr. Churchill called "the bubble and effervescence of
new movements," were it not clear that they had left a
lasting residue behind them, a definite and clear improvement in the relations between priests, clergymen and Free
Church ministers, a new consideration and a greater
courtesy.[153]

The system of parallel meetings had the advantage that each
of them could be more fully confessional and could maintain
a note of worship and public prayer. John Murray, S. J., has
pointed out that the cooperation was not "official co-operation
between the Catholic Church of England plus the various
Free Churches."[154] Rather, it was the collaboration of individual Catholics with individuals of the various denominations; with the approval of their respective authorities, they
"attempted to work with one another along certain specified
lines. . . ."[155] To the good results of the cooperation must

---

[152] *Ibid.,* 7.
[153] Woodruff, "The First Ten Years," *op. cit.,* 37.
[154] "The Story of Co-operation," *op. cit.,* 44.
[155] *Ibid.*

be added the fact that Christian principles were recognized as the basis of social and economic problems and of international affairs.

In the postwar years, Christian cooperation assumed an international aspect. Close relations were "maintained with the *Christian News-Letter* and with the Protestant World Agency at Geneva (the International Christian Press and Information Service), as well as with the British Council of Churches. . . ."[156] This transfer of interest was in keeping with other postwar innovations in the Sword of the Spirit.

Postwar Developments. Cardinal Hinsley's death in March, 1943, removed a dynamic and compelling leadership from the Sword of the Spirit movement. However, with the advent of Archbishop Griffin to the presidency in February, 1944, new vigor and new directions revivified the crusade of prayer, study, and action. The fundamental aims of the society remained unaltered, but under the leadership of Archbishop Griffin the international dimension of the movement came ever more clearly in focus. Building on the foundation erected by his predecessor in the study of the Pope's five peace points, in the Christian approach to foreign soldiers in England and to refugees from the war-torn, persecution-ridden countries of the Continent, in the formation of Polish, French, Belgian, and Czech Sword units among the refugees, and in the establishment of Sword branches abroad, he centered attention on international problems. His first directive as president was to work for the revival and restoration of the common life of Europe, "i.e., a common, accepted, standard of values; a common view of man's purpose and destiny, of his rights and duties."[157] To make such a directive

[156] "Annual Report for 1945–1946," *The Sword,* No. 98 (October, 1946) , 5.

[157] "Role of the Movement," *The Sword of the Spirit,* Bulletin No. 75 (November, 1944), 1. The article is the president's address read at the annual general meeting.

practicable on the national level, a five-point program for study, prayer, and action was suggested:

1. . . .we must base our actions on the principles of justice and charity. . . .
2. We must try to restore a sense of security among other peoples. . . .
3. . . . we must make greater efforts in trying to understand the traditions and the standards of life of other peoples. . . .
4. It will also mean a more equitable distribution in the world's goods. . . .
5. We shall also have to try to restore confidence between nations. . . .
Finally, and to sum up, we really want to restore Europe as a family of nations.[158]

National problems and issues were not to be neglected; Christian international unity could be built only on Christian national unity. And for this the fundamental human liberties, especially those of the family, were stressed. The movement was to study every government proposal in social and international legislation and, when possible, issue pamphlets on the government white papers.[159] In this way the Sword of the Spirit could help to inform Catholics of the right principles according to which national affairs should be regulated, and could make "Catholics realise that they must take their fair share in politics, in Trade Unions, in local government, and in national movements. . . ."[160]

"What is the task of The Sword of the Spirit now that the war is over?"[161] and ". . . . we need *new aims* and a *new*

[158] *Ibid.*, 2.

[159] "Annual Report for 1944–45," *The Sword of the Spirit,* Bulletin No. 86 (October, 1945), 5.

[160] Archbishop Griffin, "The Council Meeting," *The Sword of the Spirit,* Bulletin No. 80 (April, 1945), 3.

[161] "Power of Spirit—or Spirit of Power," *The Sword,* No. 89 (January, 1949), 1.

spirit . . .[162] indicated the opinion of Christopher Dawson, Vice-President of the movement, when faced with the period of reconstruction. Cardinal Griffin, the executive committee and the council fully realized that a revised statement of aims was necessary "in order to relate the general object of the Movement more precisely to post-war conditions."[163] A memorandum was therefore submitted at the Low Week meeting of the hierarchy of England and Wales in 1947 for approval or modifications, and the help of bishops was solicited to increase membership in the movement. With the requested approbation, the new statement of aims was published in May, 1947.

The fundamental object today is to defend the Church. Its method is to inform Catholics and all other Christians about the issues confronting the Catholic religion in so many countries by publications, meetings, study circles, etc., with a view to producing a laity both educated and active over these questions, and capable of explaining the basic principles of international order as taught by the Holy See.[164]

This provided a broad, comprehensive basis for the post-war endeavors of the Sword of the Spirit. That it left doubt as to definite, practicable goals the movement was to pursue was evinced by a series of resolutions presented by the northern groups' conference and passed at the annual general meeting, November 22, 1947. Three of the resolutions were directly relevant to the problem of implementing the statement of aims:

Resolution 1.—That The Sword of the Spirit should adhere closely to the Preamble in its Constitution which

---

162 *Ibid.,* 2.
163 "The Hierarchy and the Sword of the Spirit," *The Sword,* No. 105 (May, 1947), 3.
164 *Ibid.,* 4.

reads: "The Movement of the Sword of the Spirit was founded by Cardinal Hinsley (Aug. 1, 1940) and is a Movement consecrated to building up an informed and articulate Christian public opinion on National and International affairs"; That the activities of The Sword should be evenly balanced between National and International affairs.

. . . .

Resolution 2.—That there be a clearly defined and distinctive line the Sword of the Spirit must take to put its case and cause to the Catholic community in this country.

. . . .

Resolution 3.—That the National Executive explore fully the question of training members as Leaders on the lines of the R.A.F. Guild Leadership Courses or on the ordered Study Plans in use in the C.E.G. and C.S.G.[165]

In reality, the immediate postwar years saw a general decline in Sword activity. Lectures, meetings, and retreats continued but with less enthusiasm, attendance, and frequency. Local activities were stalled, seemingly lost in confusion and frustration as to what to do. In 1950, at an extraordinary general meeting of the Sword of the Spirit, Cardinal Griffin again set the movement on the path of expansion and deep interest by presenting a practicable program that coincided with the need to stimulate and "to promote the spiritual and intellectual life of Catholics."[166] Succinct and clear is the following summary of what the program included:

The wide general aims remain and the Cardinal has now given us precise and definite work to do. He wants us to study the life of the Church today and interpret it for the mass of our people, having particular regard to the social and political action of Catholics on the continent. Further,

---

[165] "The Annual General Meeting," *The Sword*, No. 110 (December, 1947), 21–22.

[166] "An Imperative Need," *Social Justice Review*, L (November, 1950), 232.

he directs us to interest ourselves in the work of the United Nations and other great international bodies, measuring their activities against our Christian standards. He commends a work of charity to us, in the care of the tens of thousands of exiles from Europe, now to be integrated into our community. He wants to see this done throughout the country at large with more decentralisation and more working from the parish unit. And he wants us to be powerful in the land for the spreading of Catholic truth, the word of God.[167]

Gradually the Sword of the Spirit became more exclusively oriented to international affairs, where it met a need that was not filled by any other Catholic organization. By 1954 it had lost its character of a mass movement, and was considered "a centre for diffusing information on matters affecting the Church throughout the world, and for rallying Catholic public opinion to action when necessary."[168] Its official organ became the bimonthly *Catholic International Outlook,* a correspondence information service that was "used by a number of Catholic newspapers overseas, as well as by clergy and laity in this country and abroad."[169] When Cardinal Griffin died in 1956, the Sword of the Spirit was well established according to the "new charter" which he had given it six years before. His successor, Archbishop Godfrey, was well aware of the significant role the Sword of the Spirit was playing on behalf of the Catholic Church, and declared: "It is not my intention to depart in any way from the directive given by my predecessor."[170]

Incontrovertibly the Sword of the Spirit contributed

---

[167] Agnellus Andrew, O.F.M., "A New Campaign," *The Sword,* XI (September, 1950), 33.

[168] "The Sword of the Spirit," *The Tablet,* CCIV (July 10, 1957), 21.

[169] "The Sword of the Spirit," *The Tablet,* CCX (July 6, 1957), 21.

[170] *Ibid.*

notably to the Social Catholic movement in the period 1940–1955. However, one opinion is that it did not achieve its potential influence for two reasons: (1.) The Catholics in 1940 were not ready for the lead which Cardinal Hinsley tried to give them; they were too insular and unaware of their responsibilities as members of a universal Church; (2.) The movement was weakened by the fact that Cardinal Hinsley began it without consulting his fellow bishops. The implication, and assumption of non-Catholics, that the Cardinal had jurisdiction over the whole island and could launch a national movement on his own, made many bishops withhold their support.[171] Consequently, while it was essentially a Catholic action movement, in many areas it could not be so considered officially because it lacked the respective bishop's mandate. Undoubtedly, Cardinal Hinsley was ahead of his time in his idea of Christian unity. Now, almost a generation later, the possibility of unity in a pluralistic society is just beginning to be recognized.

---

[171] Woodruff, "The First Ten Years," *op. cit.,* 37–38.

Chapter V

CONCLUSION

As reiterated throughout this study, the primary purpose of the Social Catholic movement in England was to produce a leavening force which would permeate society and direct the political, economic, and social changes and developments along Christian principles. Work and effort of such nature will scarcely produce statistics to prove or disprove the effectiveness of the endeavors. That something was accomplished is irrefutable, and although the spiritual content of the achievements prohibits exact measurement, some general observations may, nevertheless, be made.

It has already been indicated in the study in what areas the greatest influence of the Social Catholic movement was exerted. The beneficial results are evident, particularly through economic and social legislation for the last twenty-five years of the study, not so much in the superstructure as in the underpinnings. At times the underpinnings appear insecure, threatening to disintegrate in the flood waters of un-christian attitudes. But when a crisis arises, and Catholics are roused by the attacks upon their basic standards, then the foundations are reinforced and the principles stand firm and unyielding.

The Social Catholic movement waxed and waned according to circumstances in the country and, to some extent, to leadership within the movement. These very facts are indicative of the lack of understanding among Catholics of their social responsibilities and of the lack of knowledge of

Catholic principles and how they were to be applied under all circumstances. Often this was a culpable ignorance stemming from a general apathy among Catholics. Enthusiasm was aroused only spasmodically. What was accomplished cannot be attributed to any one person or organization but rather to a profusion of local, regional, and national undertakings. Nevertheless, special influence was exerted by the Catholic Social Guild through its many years of persistent efforts in the written word and in its ramifications of summer schools, study clubs, and the Catholic Workers' College.

While England ascribes much of its social welfare program to the Beveridge Report, it has a Christian hue, embodying some tenets of the social encyclicals and some of the Christian principles advocated by the Social Catholic movement. The constant agitation for reforms in economic areas, emphasized at intervals by the revival of the Associations of Catholic Trade Unionists, and in social areas for particular needs, e.g., housing, could not continue without some recognition by the government. Furthermore, the few but articulate Catholic members of the House of Commons[1] did not hesitate to uphold Christian principles on whatever issues arose.

In the political realm two achievements in particular can be credited to a considerable degree to the Social Catholic movement. With the large number of Catholics in the Labor party the movement was able to help steer the party clear of continental socialism. The anti-Christian tenet embodied in the Constitution of 1918 was never activated, and Cardinal Bourne and his successors declared unequivocally that Catholics were free to join any of the major parties in England.

---

[1] Probably the most outstanding member was Christopher Hollis. Being a Conservative, he did not give wholehearted approval to all social legislation. However, he did not sit by in approval of the violation of Catholic principles.

They fully supported the Social Catholic movement in its second political achievement also, viz., prevention of the formation of a Catholic political party. Catholics were to become active, articulate members of the existing parties and endeavor to direct them along Christian policies and principles.

Obstacles to the Social Catholic movement were numerous, and some of the most devastating were those set up by the Catholics themselves. Two examples were the Back-to-the-Land movement and the Distributist movement. In Chapter IV it was pointed out how impractical the former was and how its advocates failed to keep in line with the thinking of the Church on economic matters. The Church did not condemn the capitalistic system, yet in both these movements the aim was to establish a new economic system, particularly in the sense of the Distributist state. The movement was wholly unrealistic and drew upon the group, as well as upon the Church, the ridicule of the practical-minded and far-sighted. The Social Catholic movement had previously been accused of being too theoretical; Distributism, with its highly romantic ideas, discredited it immeasurably more. Papal works[2] might be quoted indefinitely to substantiate the Church's realistic, practical approach to economic problems and its inferred opposition to such utopian system as Distributism. Able Catholic writers, supporting Distributism, frittered away their talent, destroyed their potential influence, and by misrepresentation of its teachings caused the Church to be considered a benighted institution, unfit for the modern progressive generation.

Perhaps the greatest hindrance to further success of the

---

[2] *Mater et Magistra* is a compendium of the Church's socio-economic teaching, since it includes a résumé of *Rerum Novarum, Quadragesimo Anno,* and Pius XII's radio message of Pentecost, 1941.

Social Catholic movement was the proliferation of organizations, societies, and movements in which energy and enthusiasm were dissipated by being spread too thinly, or in which the extensive overlapping of interests and work led to confusion and an inevitable lack of responsibility in any one area. Most significant of this was the elaborate organization of Catholic action on a nation-wide, diocesan scale in 1936, and the launching of the Sword of the Spirit movement a few years later. While Cardinal Hinsley, from the outset, viewed the latter as an international movement, the immediate reality of it was on a national, diocesan basis, involving the same personnel on which Catholic action had relied for its leadership. In its early years it dealt with many of the same problems on which Catholic action had focused its attention. Similar situations prevailed within dioceses and within parishes. A lack of persistent concentration upon any one phase was unavoidable under such circumstances.

This is not to deny the Church's principle of unity in diversity, by which she seeks to avoid the stereotype and at the same time to encourage creativity and initiative to enable man to fulfill his destiny according to the Providence of God. Nor is it to advocate the amalgamation of all societies, or to suggest that the Social Catholic movement be carried on in the hierarchical scheme employed by the Communists.[3] Rather, the writer sees the need for a central, coordinating organization to effect concerted action and mutual help among existing bodies. The diversity of societies seems necessary, since they cater to a "variety of class, interest, temperament and inclination,"[4] and, taking into account the vagaries of human nature,

---

[3] There were individuals who advocated this system, e.g., see C. L. McDermott, "There's War On," *The Christian Democrat,* new ser., I (December, 1950), 274–278.

[4] T. Cummins, "Any Questions?" *The Christian Democrat,* new ser., V (July–August, 1955), 422–423.

if there were an amalgamation, the membership of the joint body would suffer considerably and break-away societies would be formed again on the old pattern. You cannot stop people forming societies and it would be difficult to force societies already in existence to deviate from their own purposes, which may be similar but are rarely identical with those of others.[5]

Closer liaison between societies and organizations, coupled with a lively understanding and knowledge among Catholics of their social responsibility, appears to be the way to greater success for the Social Catholic movement. That the former is lacking has been indicated previously; that the latter is also lacking is apparent from the dearth of lay leaders in the Social Catholic movement, from the static number of converts per annum, and from the persistent "leakage" problem, all of which have held the statistical strength of the Church in England at approximately the same level through the years under consideration in this study. The Catholic layman has not assumed his rightful place in the apostolic work of the Church. Since 1925 the yearly adult conversions have averaged 12,000 to 13,000, yet the total Catholic population has made an increase of scarcely one million while the entire population grew by approximately seven million.[6] Writing in 1959, William Lawson stated that "the proportion of children leaving Catholic schools who at once lapse from the faith is between seventy and ninety per cent."[7] The percentage was not equally high in all areas, and some returned to the Church in later years. Accurate statistical information on these topics is difficult to ascertain, but the trends are well indicated. General apathy and indifference appear to

---

[5] *Ibid.*

[6] Statistics taken from *Catholic Directory,* 1956.

[7] "Any Questions?" *The Christian Democrat,* new ser. (May, 1959), 303.

characterize aptly the Catholicism of mid-twentieth-century England.

Through all the vicissitudes of the Social Catholic movement, through its seeming failures, through all the facets of its endeavors, there has accrued to the Church in England a good—immeasurable but plainly cognizable, intangible but unmistakable—that may yet serve as the basis for a more complete triumph of the Social Catholic movement. This "good" is the respect and prestige that the Catholic church holds in modern England. Its members do not cower in fear of oppressive legislation. There is a new independence and self-confidence in its dealings with the state, and it speaks out with a clarity and confidence very different from the uncertain sound of a century earlier.[8] It takes a firm grip on the problems of the day, and intelligent men can no longer profitably ignore the Catholic Church's views on them. Writing in 1950, Michael de La Bedoyere recorded an incident which graphically portrays this new public recognition of the Catholic church:

> Now in recent weeks something very unusual and startling has happened. For days on end the best space in this unique column in British journalism seems to have been handed over to Christianity—indeed to Catholicism—not even "Roman Catholicism" in a paper which used to refer to the Cardinal as "the Roman Catholic Archbishop of Westminster."
>
> It all began with a long feature article in the *Times*, called "Catholicism Today"—or rather it seems to have begun earlier. A few weeks before, the English Carmelites recovered the historic Aylesford Priory where St. Simon Stock once lived. . . .
>
> Rather surprisingly, this event was made the subject of a fine leading article in the *Times*, which, in commenting

---

[8] Michael P. Fogarty contends that this is true of the Protestant churches also and in all free countries (*Christian Democracy in Western Europe 1820–1953*, pp. 420–421).

on the wheel of fortune, pointed out how old sectarian controversies had so much died down that everyone could greet the return of the Friars to their historic home.

.   .   .   .   .   .

This provocative article ["Catholicism Today"] which, I repeat, was very friendly in tone throughout . . . was followed by letter after letter, often given the enviable top place in the column, signed by Catholic and Anglican, Bishops, Jesuits and Benedictines and parsons, a Member of Parliament, and notable lay spokesmen, both Catholic and non-Catholic. Nothing like this had happened for years.[9]

It is in the light of this recognition that present-day and future leaders in the Social Catholic movement can hope for even greater success.

---

[9] "From My Window in Fleet Street," *The Catholic World*, CLXX (January, 1950), 304–305.

BIBLIOGRAPHY

PRIMARY SOURCES

Books

BELLOC, HILAIRE. *The Catholic Church and the Principle of Private Property.* London: Catholic Truth Society, 1920.

———. *The Restoration of Property.* New York: Sheed & Ward, 1936.

———. *The Servile State.* First American edition. New York: Henry Holt and Company, 1946. (First English edition, 1912).

CHESTERTON, GILBERT KEITH. *Do We Agree?* Hartford, Connecticut: Edwin V. Mitchell, 1928.

———. *The Outline of Sanity.* New York: Dodd, Mead & Company, 1927.

CLUMP, CYRIL C. *The Economic and Political Life of Man.* Oxford: Catholic Social Guild, 1947.

GILL, ERIC. *Autobiography.* New York: The Devin-Adair Company, 1942.

———. *Sacred & Secular etc.* London: J. M. Dent & Sons, Ltd., for Hague and Gill, Ltd., 1940.

———. *Work and Property.* London: J. M. Dent & Sons, Ltd., 1937.

GORDON, ANDREW, S.J. *Security, Freedom and Happiness.* Oxford: Samuel Walker, Ltd., 1948.

MANNING, HENRY EDWARD. *Miscellanies.* Vol. II. London: Burns and Oates, 1877.

McNABB, VINCENT, O.P. *The Church and the Land.* London: Burns, Oates & Washbourne, Ltd., 1926.

———. *Old Principles and the New Order.* New York: Sheed & Ward, 1942.

McQUILLAN, JOHN, *et al. Flee to the Fields.* London: Heath Cranton, Ltd., 1934.

207

Planned Social Study. Oxford: Catholic Social Guild, 1946.
PRIDGEON, CHARLES, S.J. *Opportunity for Trade Unionists*. Revised edition. Oxford: Catholic Social Guild, 1950.

Articles and Periodicals

BEALES, A. C. F. "The Sword of the Spirit," *The Month,* CLXXVI (October, 1940), 203–208.
Catholic Social Yearbook. Oxford: Catholic Social Guild, 1920–1959. (Not published in 1950.)
CHESTERTON, GILBERT KEITH. "Distributism Again," *Commonweal,* XVI (October 12, 1932), 551–552.
The Christian Democrat. Oxford: Catholic Social Guild, old ser., 1920–1943; new ser. 1950–1960.
CRANE, PAUL, S.J. "Current Comment," *Christian Order,* I (March, 1960), 151–161.
CRAWFORD, VIRGINIA M. "The Coming of Age of the C.S.G.," *Studies* (September, 1930), 456–466.
The Cross and the Plough. Organ of the Catholic Land Associations of England and Wales. X (Christmas, 1943); XI (Ladyday, 1944); XII (Michaelmas, 1945; Christmas, 1945); XV (Ladyday, 1948; Michaelmas, 1948; Christmas, 1948); XVI (Ladyday, 1949).
G. K.'s Weekly. 1925–1936.
JEBB, REGINALD. "Private Property and the Distributist Thesis," *Blackfriars,* XXXI (July, 1950), 324–330.
SOMERVILLE, HENRY. "The Catholic Social Movement in England," *The Catholic Charities Review,* XIII (March, 1929), 81–82.
The Sword of the Spirit. 1940–1946.
The Sword. 1946–1948; 1950–1952.
The Tablet. 1920–1959. Not directly a primary source for the topic, but indispensable for contemporary comment and interpretation.

Reports

The Catholic Workers' College. *Report for the Year, 1948–49* (July 31, 1949).
———. *Report for the Year, 1949–50* (July, 1950).
Declaration of Trust in Reference to the Catholic Workers' College (November 4, 1925).

Catholic Social Guild. *Report of the Seventeenth Annual Meeting* (July 25, 1926). Includes report of the Catholic Workers' College and statutes of the C.S.G.

------. *Report of the Thirty-Fifth Annual Meeting* (July 30, 1944.)

------. *Report of the Thirty-Sixth Annual Meeting* (July 29, 1945).

Statutes of the Catholic Social Guild. Revised and approved at the 1949 annual general meeting.

Catholic Social Guild Leaflets

"The Catholic Social Guild: What it Is, and What it Does," n.d.

CRANE, PAUL, S.J. "First Things First," No. 30, 1948.

GIBSON, J. N. "The Housing Problem," No. 35, 1949.

"Human Rights." No. 26, 1948.

LUCEY, CORNELIUS, D.D. "The Ethics of Nationalization," No. 13, 1947.

SANDERSON, SAMUEL. "Reflections on National Insurance," No. 21, 1948.

SARMIENTO, DOROTHY. "A Social Worker Looks at the National Health Service," No. 27, 1948.

WALSH, ROBERT P. "Counter Attack in the Unions," No. 16, 1947.

SECONDARY SOURCES

Books

ATTWATER, DONALD (ed.). *A Catholic Dictionary.* 3rd ed. New York: The Macmillan Company, 1958.

------. *Modern Christian Revolutionaries.* New York: The Devin-Adair Company, 1947.

BALDWIN, GEORGE B. *Beyond Nationalization.* Cambridge, Massachusetts: Harvard University Press, 1955.

BECK, GEORGE ANDREW, D.D. (ed.). *The English Catholics 1850–1950.* London: Burns, Oates, 1950.

BROWNE, HENRY, S.J. *The Catholic Evidence Movement.* London: Burns, Oates & Washbourne, Ltd., 1921.

The Catholic Directory. 1926 and 1956. London: Burns, Oates & Washbourne, Ltd.

CLEARY, J. M. *Catholic Social Action in Britain, 1909–1959.* Oxford: Catholic Social Guild, 1961.

209

CIVARDI, LUIGI. *A Manual of Catholic Action.* Translated by C. C. MARTINDALE, S.J. New York: Sheed & Ward, Inc., 1936.

COLE, G. D. H. and POSTGATE, RAYMOND. *The British People 1746–1946.* New York: Alfred A. Knopf, 1947.

COURT, WILLIAM H. B. *Coal.* London: His Majesty's Stationery Office and Longmans, Green and Co., 1951.

CROFTS, A. M. *Catholic Social Action.* London: Alexander Ouseley, Ltd., 1936.

DERRY, THOMAS K. and JARMAN, T. L. *The Making of Modern Britain.* New York: New York University Press, 1956.

ECKSTEIN, HARRY, *The English Health Service.* Cambridge, Massachusetts: Harvard University Press, 1958.

FANFANI, AMINTORE. *Catechism of Catholic Social Teaching.* Translated by HENRY J. YANNONE from the third edition. Westminster, Maryland: The Newman Press, 1960.

FLANDERS, ALAN. *Trade Unions.* New York: Hutchinson's University Library, 1952.

FOGARTY, MICHAEL P. *Christian Democracy in Western Europe 1820–1953.* Notre Dame, Indiana: University of Notre Dame Press, 1957.

FREEMANTLE, ANNE (ed.). *The Papal Encyclicals.* New York: The New American Library, 1956.

GURIAN, WALDEMAR and FITZSIMMONS, MATTHEW A. *The Catholic Church and World Affairs.* Notre Dame, Indiana: University of Notre Dame Press, 1954.

HALL, MARY PENELOPE. *The Social Services of Modern England.* 2nd ed. Revised. London: Routledge & Kegan Paul Ltd., 1953.

HAYNES, WILLIAM WARREN. *Nationalization in Practice.* Boston: Graduate School of Business Administration, Harvard University, 1953.

HEENAN, JOHN G. *Cardinal Hinsley.* London: Burns, Oates & Washbourne, Ltd., 1944.

HUSSLEIN, JOSEPH, S.J. *Social Wellsprings.* Vol. II. Milwaukee: The Bruce Publishing Company, 1942.

KENYON, RUTH. *The Catholic Faith and the Industrial Order.* London: Philip Alan, 1931.

KIERNAN, EDWARD J. *Arthur J. Penty: His Contribution to So-*

cial Thought. Washington, D.C.: The Catholic University of America Press, 1941.

KOTHEN, ROBERT. *La pensée et l'action sociales des catholiques 1789–1941.* Louvain: Em. Warny (Imprimeur-Editeur), 1945.

LATOURETTE, KENNETH SCOTT. *The Twentieth Century in Europe.* Vol. IV: *Christianity in a Revolutionary Age.* 1st ed. New York: Harper & Brothers, 1961.

LESLIE, SHANE. *Cardinal Manning.* New York: P. J. Kenedy & Sons, 1954.

———. *The Oxford Movement 1833–1933.* Milwaukee: The Bruce Publishing Company, 1933.

MATHEW, DAVID, D.D. *Catholicism in England 1535–1935.* New York: Longmans, Green and Co., 1936.

MCENTEE, GEORGIANA PUTNAM. *The Social Catholic Movement in Great Britain.* New York: The Macmillan Company, 1927.

MILLER, RAYMOND J. *Forty Years After: Pius XI and the Social Order.* St. Paul, Minnesota: Radio Replies Press, 1947.

MILNE-BAILEY, WALTER. *Trade Unionism and the State.* London: George Allen & Unwin, Ltd., 1934.

NEWMAN, JEREMIAH. *What Is Catholic Action?* Westminster, Maryland: The Newman Press, 1958.

O'CONNOR, DANIEL A. *Catholic Social Doctrine.* Westminster, Maryland: The Newman Press, 1956.

OLDMEADOW, ERNEST. *Francis Cardinal Bourne,* 2 vols. London: Burns, Oates & Washbourne, Ltd., 1940.

REYNOLDS, ERNEST EDWIN. *Three Cardinals.* New York: P. J. Kenedy & Sons, 1958.

SCHWEINITZ, KARL DE. *England's Road to Social Security.* Philadelphia: University of Pennsylvania Press, 1943.

SHEWRING, WALTER (ed.). *Letters of Eric Gill.* New York: The Devin-Adair Company, 1948.

SOMERVILLE, HENRY. *Studies in the Catholic Social Movement.* London: Burns, Oates & Washbourne, Ltd., 1933.

SPEAIGHT, ROBERT. *The Life of Hilaire Belloc.* New York: Farrar, Straus & Cudahy, 1957.

STEWARD, J. D. *British Pressure Groups.* Oxford: Clarendon Press, 1958.

211

STURMTHAL, ADOLPH FOX. *Unity and Diversity in European Labor*. Glencoe, Illinois: The Free Press, 1953.

TITMUSS, RICHARD MORRIS. *Essays on the Welfare State*. New Haven: Yale University Press, 1959.

VALENTINE, FERDINAND, O.P. *Father Vincent McNabb, O.P.* Westminster, Maryland: The Newman Press, 1955.

WARD, MAISIE. *Gilbert Keith Chesterton*. New York: Sheed & Ward, 1943.

———. *Return to Chesterton*. New York: Sheed & Ward, 1952.

WARD, MAISIE and SHEED, FRANK J. *Catholic Evidence Training Outlines*. 4th ed. New York: Sheed & Ward, 1943.

WATKINS, E. I. *Roman Catholicism in England from the Reformation to 1950*. New York: Oxford University Press, 1957.

WEBSTER, RICHARD A. *The Cross and the Fasces*. Stanford, California: Stanford University Press, 1960.

WHITAKER, JOSEPH. *An Almanac for 1961*. London: J. Whitaker & Sons, Ltd.

YZERMANS, VINCENT A. *The Major Addresses of Pope Pius XII*. Vol. II: *Christmas Messages*. St. Paul, Minnesota: The North Central Publishing Company, 1961.

Articles

ARMSTRONG, A. H. "Catholics and the University," *Blackfriars*, XXXII (July–August, 1951), 334–339.

ATTWATER, DONALD. "The Decline of Distributism," *Commonweal*, LIII (February 2, 1951), 421–422.

BARNES, JAMES. "Fascism and the Catholic Church," *The Dublin Review*, CLXXV (July, August, September, 1924), 93–101.

———. "Fascism and the International Centre of Fascist Studies," *The Dublin Review*, CLXXXV (October, November, December, 1929), 264–281.

BEDOYERE, MICHAEL DE LA. "From My Window in Fleet Street," *The Catholic World*, CLXX (January, 1950), 303–306.

———. "From My Window in Fleet Street," *The Catholic World*, CLXXIX (April, 1954), 56–61.

"Britain's Cradle to Grave Security," *America*, LXXIX (July 17, 1948), 338.

212

BYRNE, JAMES. "Catholic Evidence Guild," *The Catholic Encyclopedia,* Vol. XVII, Supplement I. Ed. VINCENT C. HOPKINS, S.J. New York: The Encyclopedia Press, Inc., 1922, pp. 165–166.

"Carmel" and "This Leakage," *The Month,* CLXI (June, 1933) , 493–502

"Catholic Truth Society," *The New Catholic Dictionary.* Ed. CONDE B. PALLEN and JOHN J. WYNNE, S.J. (1929), p. 184.

"Catholic Young Men's Society," *The Catholic Encyclopedia Dictionary.* New York: The Gilmary Society (1941), p. 1031.

"Christian Rejuvenation," *Blackfriars,* XXV (October, 1944) , 361–365.

CLAYTON, JOSEPH. "Christian Tradition in the English Labour Movement," *Blackfriars,* XIX (April, 1938) , 244–249.

COLLINS, EDWARD, S.J. "Distributism," *The Irish Monthly,* LXXII (January, 1944) , 5–16.

"Conference of Catholic Evidence Guild," *The Catholic World,* CXXXIV (December, 1931) , 364–365.

"Conference of Lausanne," *Encyclopedia Britannica,* Vol. XIII (1960) , pp. 772–773.

DERRICK, MICHAEL. "The Conversion of England," *The Catholic World,* CLXXXII (March, 1956) , 436–444.

"Ditchling's Twentieth Century Guild Colony," *The Catholic World,* CXXXV (August, 1932) , 598–600.

DONNELLY, JOSEPH F. "Cooperation for Civic Goals," *The Catholic Mind,* LII (November, 1954) , 675–677.

"The Failure of 'Back to the Land,'" *Blackfriars,* XXVII (December, 1946) , 473–475.

FORSTER, THOMAS. "A Catholic Housing Programme," *Blackfriars,* XIV (April, 1933) , 248–256.

"The Future of the Catholic Land Movement," *The Month,* CLXI (March, 1933) , 204.

GAFFNEY, MAURICE. "Social Guild Summer School," *The Irish Monthly,* LXXIX (November, 1951) , 471–476.

GWYNN, DENIS. "Cardinal Bourne," *The Sign,* XIV (March, 1935) 490–491.

———. "Catholic England Under King George V," *The Catholic World,* CXLIII (April, 1936) , 68–75.

HOLLIS, CHRISTOPHER. "The Case for the Distributist State," *Ave Maria,* new ser., XLVIII (December 17, 1938) 769–772.

HOPE, CHARLES. "Ferment in England," *The Catholic World,* CLXVII (August, 1948), 410–414.

HUMPHRIES, SILVESTER, O.P. "The Servile State Reconsidered," *Blackfriars,* XIV (May, 1933), 354–357.

"An Imperative Need," *Social Justice Review,* XLIII (November, 1950), 232–233.

JEWELL, WALTER. "The Catholic Evidence Guild," *The Catholic Encyclopedia,* Vol. XVIII, Supplement II. Ed. VINCENT C. HOPKINS, S.J. New York: The Encyclopedia Press, Inc., 1958, n.p.

KEATING, JOSEPH, S.J., "After the Great Strike," *The Month,* CXLVII (June, 1926), 481–493.

KENNEDY, WILLIAM F. "The Third Way: A New Economics," *The Commonweal,* LIV (April 13, 1951), 14–16.

LAND, PHILIP S., S.J. "Colin Clark on the Welfare State," *Social Order,* new ser., IV (October, 1954), 354–356.

LESLIE, SHANE. "Cardinal Manning and the London Strike of 1889," *The Dublin Review,* CLXVII (October, November, December, 1920), 219–231.

LION, ALINE. "The Economic Life of Fascist Italy," *The Dublin Review,* (January, February, March, 1928), 59–72.

LORD, IDDESLEIGH. "A Catholic in Politics," *Blackfriars,* XXXII (March, 1951), 101–107.

MCEVOY, HUBERT. "The Catholic Action Society," *The Month,* CLVII (June, 1931), 507–516.

MANSFIELD, M. "The Church and the Hour of Fascism," *The Dublin Review,* CLXXXI (July, 1927), 51–66.

MASSE, BENJAMIN L. "Sword of Spirit Drawn for Christian Order," *America,* LXVIII (March 20, 27, 1943), 649–650, 682–683.

"The Nationalization of the Mines," *Blackfriars,* VII (July, 1926), 395–397.

"Progress of the C.T.S.," *The Month,* CLVI (November, 1930), 461.

REEVES, JOHN BAPTIST. "A Coming of Age," *Blackfrairs,* XI (September, 1930), 519–527.

Ryan, William F., S.J. "C.S.G. and the Welfare State," *Social Order*, new ser., V (June, 1955) , 265–270.

Shove, Herbert. "Fascism and Religion," *The Catholic Mind*, XXXII (March 22, 1934) , 119–120.

Stancioff, Marion Mitchell. "Distributism," *Integrity*, III (March, 1949) , 3–15.

"The Stoll Meetings," *The Month*, CLXXVII (May-June, 1941) , 193–201.

"Sword of the Spirit," *The Commonweal*, XXXIV (October 17, 1941) 614–617.

"The Sword of the Spirit," *Social Justice Review*, L (September, 1957) , 158.

Synnott, Finbar. "Progress of the Y.C.W.," *Blackfriars*, XIX (October, 1938) , 762–764.

Todd, John. "Distributism," *Blackfriars*, XXX (June, 1949) , 273–282.

———. "The Leakage Problem in England," *Integrity*, IX (September, 1955) , 38–43.

"Topics of the Month," *The Month*, CXXXVII (May, 1921) , 458–462; CXXXVIII (July, 1921) , 75–78; CXLVII (May, 1926) , 461–464; (June, 1926) , 549–552; CXLVIII (August, 1926) , 176–178; (November, 1926) , 457–460.

Trevett, Reginald F. "A Catholic People's College," *Blackfriars*, XXVI (May, 1945) , 186–191.

"Two Views of Nationalization," *The Commonweal*, XLIX (March 4, 1949) , 519–520.

Walsh, Robert P. "A Fifty Years Plan," *Blackfriars*, XVIII (November, 1937) , 857–859.

———. "Catholic Action in England," *The Ecclesiastical Review*, C (March, 1939) , 260–264.

———. "The British A.C.T.U.," *Social Justice Review*, XL (March, 1948) , 371–373.

Watt, Louis, S.J. "Sympathetic Strikes," *The Month*, CL (July, 1927) , 18–27.

———. "Christianity and Socialism," *The Clergy Review*, new ser., XXVI (August, 1946) , 437–438.

Woollen, C. J. "Parents' Associations in England," *Blackfriars*, XXV (August, 1944) , 294–299.

———. "A Solution of the Leakage," *Blackfriars,* XXVII (March, 1946) , 96–99.

Unpublished Material

BARRETT, PATRICIA, R.S.C.J. "The Social Catholic Movement in England From 1850 to 1940." Unpublished Master's thesis, St. Louis University, 1940.